The Pieces Join

The Pieces Join

Navigating Faith, Trauma and Recovery

Beth Keith

© Beth Keith 2026
First published in 2026 by the Canterbury Press Norwich

Editorial office
3rd Floor, Invicta House
110 Golden Lane,
London EC1Y 0TG, UK
www.canterburypress.co.uk

Canterbury Press is an imprint of Hymns Ancient & Modern Ltd
(a registered charity)

Hymns Ancient & Modern® is a registered trademark of
Hymns Ancient & Modern Ltd
13A Hellesdon Park Road, Norwich,
Norfolk NR6 5DR, UK

All rights reserved. No part of this publication may be reproduced,
stored in a retrieval system, or transmitted,
in any form or by any means, electronic, mechanical,
photocopying or otherwise, without the prior permission of
the publisher, Canterbury Press.

Beth Keith has asserted her right under the Copyright, Designs and Patents Act
1988 to be identified as the Author of this Work

British Library Cataloguing in Publication data
A catalogue record for this book is available from the British Library

ISBN: 978-1-78622-601-3

EU GPSR Authorized Representative
LOGOS EUROPE, 9 rue Nicolas Poussin, 17000, LA ROCHELLE, France
E-mail: Contact@logoseurope.eu

Scripture quotations are from New Revised Standard Version Bible: Anglicized
Edition, copyright © 1989, 1995 National Council of the Churches of Christ in
the United States of America. Used by permission. All rights reserved worldwide.
Extracts from The Book of Common Prayer, the rights in which are vested in
the Crown, are reproduced by permission of the Crown's Patentee, Cambridge
University Press.
Extracts from *Common Worship: Services and Prayers* are copyright © The
Archbishops' Council, 2000, and are reproduced by permission. All rights
reserved. copyright@churchofengland.org
Extracts from *Common Worship: Times and Seasons* are copyright © The
Archbishops' Council, 2006, and are reproduced by permission. All rights
reserved. copyright@churchofengland.org
Extracts from *New Patterns for Worship* are copyright © The Archbishops'
Council 2002.

No part of this book may be used or reproduced in any manner for the purpose
of training artificial intelligence technologies or systems.

Typeset by Regent Typesetting
Printed and bound in Great Britain by
CPI Group (UK) Ltd

Contents

Introduction ... 1

1 Rips and Tears ... 13
2 Who Is to Blame? ... 28
3 Toxic Myths ... 38
4 Scapegoat ... 49
5 Justice ... 58
6 Perfect Victims ... 72
7 Finding Absolution ... 83
8 Forgiveness ... 97
9 Repair ... 108
10 The Pieces Join ... 121

Bibliography ... 125
Further Reading ... 129
Support Organizations ... 131

Introduction

I grew up in a well-ordered home. It's not that I was over-protected from the messiness of life; but I was brought up with the strong conviction that knowing the right things and doing the right things would result in a good life and keep any darkness away. This got me only so far…

In my 20s, I ended up working as a youth worker in the wonderful and beautiful but rough end of town. On Monday nights, we gathered at the youth centre and set the world to rights over hot chocolate and Freddos. To this point, I had kept my distance from sexual-health work. Obviously, this is part and parcel of working with teenagers; but I'd mostly managed to allow others, my loud-mouthed colleagues, to wade in where I would rather not tread. Quiet, perhaps even prudish, I felt awkward in group discussions and ill-equipped to offer much advice.

But Monday nights changed me and changed that. Over the weeks and months, it became clear – in odd comments, from tears in the corridor, in confused conversations and clear disclosures – that some of our members were victims of sexual abuse. Some had tried reporting it; but, as disabled young people, they would never count as credible witnesses, so reporting never got anywhere. Even the act of reporting was traumatic. It was messy and unclear and just the opposite of the ordered life I thought I knew. The equation that knowing the right things and doing the right things would keep you safe did not apply or make any sense here.

Over the next few years, with gifted colleagues, we worked hard, tried our best to support the young people and banged our heads against the walls of the justice system. We drew alongside, reported and sat in police stations, only to walk out in disappointment. We campaigned and found funds to set up a project aimed at supporting young disabled people at risk of sexual exploitation. We tried to bring change to youthwork policy, creating good-practice guidelines for publication. We ran workshops with disabled teenagers and their parents; and I got marginally better at talking about sex in front of a group of strangers. But any real structural or systemic change seemed like an impossible hope.

This was not the job I wanted to do. I had hoped to be a priest; but through one thing and another, I had ended up here. It was a job that was too difficult for me to do and my colleagues were much better at it than I was. It was probably a job too difficult for anyone to do for too long, though, which I guess is why so few people had done it and so few wanted to. It was too messy and hopeless and painful. I longed to leave this mess and become a priest; to find my way back to order, where knowing right things and doing right things might make sense again. But going back was not possible now.

I hadn't noticed before how the religion I knew and loved was marked out with lines and boundaries that kept it clean and holy. I had loved those lines and how they made me feel safe. But now I saw how those lines, perhaps unintentionally, had kept out those who were messy; those whose lives didn't fit that simple equation of good living; those whom I spent Monday nights with at the youth club.

Within Christianity, there is an understanding that God is present in our world and that, in the person of Jesus, we can come to know God. In the accounts of Jesus in the Gospels, we read that Jesus spent time with those who had been most excluded by society: those who were most vulnerable, most in danger. He talked about the kingdom of God being centred on the healing and restoration of those most in need. Christians are called to follow Christ and to work for this type of kingdom, this way of living; and, as we do so, we know the presence of God's Spirit with us.

As I prayed about leaving, I began to see Jesus present in the

INTRODUCTION

work I was doing: as I sat in a park with Helen, while she considered talking to the police again; as I stood in an alley, where the streetlights weren't working, and where the dark seemed to press in on every side, each step uncertain, each shadow heavy with threat. Present with Sam as she walked home, the familiar shape of her alarm pressed into one hand and her keys ready in the other. He was present at the police station, present in the tears and confusion, present in the words not spoken: present but silent; present but powerless. The more I wanted to find safety away from here, the more I wondered whether, by returning to the Church, I might leave Jesus behind. He was here, where I knew he would be, with the vulnerable, silenced and exploited. Nothing I read in the Gospels suggested that he would be anywhere else.

I don't want to romanticize this. That's the temptation: to make it sound heroic somehow. But it wasn't. It wasn't tangibly encouraging or heart-warming to know Jesus might be here, because I didn't want *here* to exist at all. And if it did, I did not want to be here. I wanted to shut my eyes against it; I wanted to find comfort in the melodies and songs telling me that Jesus loved me, and loved everybody, in a clean and ordered way. If Jesus could love the world in an ordered way, a way that kept out the dark, I could do that too. But there is little clean or ordered in Jesus' life and death. So, in the dirt and mess, I prayed. I prayed the kinds of prayer that are not formed of well-fashioned words but of tears and the gut-wrenching realization that you are just going to have to get up and carry on.

Twenty-five years have passed and I am now a priest. During the years in between, I have wrestled with these same questions and these same prayers. Do I feel any more comfortable? Probably not, but perhaps I'm more able to hold seemingly impossible beliefs together: that evil persists and that God loves. I am committed to holding on to that love without pushing away the trauma and the horror of evil, however messy and impossible that is to live with.

* * *

THE PIECES JOIN

When Judith Herman's book on trauma was published in 1992, it was seen as groundbreaking. Since then, it has shaped the way trauma has been understood and treated. When I first read her book, from among the many helpful and detailed descriptions one particular section jumped out at me. I have returned to read these sentences again and again.

> The traumatic event challenges an ordinary person to become a theologian, a philosopher, and a jurist. The survivor is called upon to articulate the values and beliefs that she once held and that the trauma destroyed. She stands mute before the emptiness of evil, feeling the insufficiency of any known system of explanation ... where all questions are reduced to one, spoken more in bewilderment than in outrage: why? The answer is beyond understanding. (Herman, 2015, p. 178)

'The traumatic event challenges an ordinary person to become a *theologian*.' It is such an odd phrase to read in a psychiatric work. But this seems to sum up my experience better than anything else. Walking alongside victims and survivors challenged my beliefs more than any religious training or experience. Later (and by then having trained as a theologian and having acquired degrees in philosophy, psychology and theology), I found my own experiences as a victim and survivor forced me to engage more urgently and deeply with the principal theological questions about God, evil, sin, forgiveness, life and death. Perhaps it should not be surprising that a faith, which carries the trauma of God at its very heart, might become more tangible through personal experiences of trauma. But trauma also carries its own incomprehensible experience; its own questions of why, with no obvious answer.

Trauma can be described (and responses and outcomes can be studied), but it is only ever really experienced first-hand. It is not something that can be chosen, nor entered as a pathway of theological study or discipleship. And yet, perhaps, those who have stood mute before the overwhelming emptiness of evil,

INTRODUCTION

and wrestled with God there, have entered those deep questions about God and have something of great worth to share.

In recent years, we have become more aware of the trauma many people carry from experiences of sexual violence. Rape Crisis estimates that 1 in 4 women and 1 in 18 men experience some type of sexual assault as adults.[1] Among children, 1 in 6 experience sexual abuse. The majority of sex crimes are not reported; for those who do report, conviction rates are far, far lower than for other crimes, leaving victims to carry the burden of this injustice.

The uncovering of crimes perpetrated by those in positions of trust, such as police officers, teachers and health-care workers, shakes our confidence in a society where this can happen. The temptation is to shut ourselves off from this reality: otherwise, we are forced to accept how poor we have been in identifying these abuses and how ill-equipped we have been to keep the most vulnerable safe.

Like other institutions, our churches are no exception. Whether it's the widespread teaching that women should remain in abusive relationships and submit to domestic violence, ministers using their positions to groom and abuse, or the alarming fact that others knew about the abuse and chose to turn away or actively covered it up, these truths remain hard to comprehend, challenging to accept and difficult to forgive. The coverage of high-profile abusers and the disclosure of abuses hidden in plain sight have shocked us into seeing what we did not want to know. No longer can we pretend that it is only happening somewhere else. No longer can we fool ourselves by saying, 'Not here, not us, not in our church, not in our community.'

The Scriptures and the pastoral practice of the Church provide wisdom and insight for helping those who have suffered trauma. However, the Church has a long and marked history of being the site of trauma, of harming rather than healing. It has a history of using Scripture, theology, preaching and worship to silence

---

[1] The Rape Crisis website outlines statistics on sexual violence in the UK: https://rapecrisis.org.uk/get-informed/statistics-sexual-violence.

victims. Much of this is done unknowingly and unintendedly; but the Church has also shielded perpetrators and invested in systems and practices to protect those in power.

Over the years, I have met, sat with, and listened to survivors. I have heard numerous accounts: each different, haunting and disturbing in its own way. I have heard about the same repeated pattern of power misused and damage inflicted. If traumatic events in general challenge survivors to become theologians, asking the big question '*Why?*', how much more so when the Church has been the site of the trauma or when the Church has intentionally shielded and colluded with those perpetrating the abuse? How can religious experiences coexist with abusive ones? How is God present here?

Victims and survivors are not a homogeneous group. Some have well-ordered lives. Others have no safe place to call home. Some are angry and hate the Church; justifiably so. Some protect themselves by keeping away and cutting off all contact. Others are active in church, supporting and leading ministries. Some have faith and are trying to work out how and if they can remain part of the church community. Some are in the early stages of disclosing what happened. Some are living in the trauma. Others are further along their journey of recovery. Some have found meaning from supporting and advocating for other victims. Some cannot find any meaning or peace.

Many victims and survivors leave the Church; but, perhaps more surprisingly, some choose to stay and report the importance of their faith in navigating a way through their experiences. For these survivors, attending church, reading the Bible and engaging in worship can be understandably problematic. How can these resources of faith, which have functioned as part of the cycle of abuse, be part of the path to recovery?

This book brings together things I have picked up along the way, from my own first-hand experience and through the accounts of others who have experienced trauma and the misuse of power within the Church. Each chapter explores different aspects of trauma and recovery; each draws on the resources of the Christian faith while also shining a light on actions and

INTRODUCTION

beliefs that can inflict further damage and inadvertently lock people into trauma rather than offering a path through.

In the past 25 years, understandings of trauma have developed and, from this, the field of trauma theology has emerged. I am grateful to the trauma specialists and theologians who have shaped my understanding and my ministerial practice. I have referred to these throughout and included various sources at the end, into which you can delve deeper if you want to. This book, while grounded in such research, is not trying to argue a case for a trauma-informed approach or explore and discuss abuse and trauma in detail; it is not trying to campaign against the injustice, though these elements are all present. Rather, this book has been written as a reflection on moving through the mess and disorientation of trauma in Christian settings. I have written this with the faces and stories of others in my mind, so I have tried to keep it concise and readable. These things are not easy to read; but I hope these words are also gentle.

* * *

The title of this book, *The Pieces Join*, comes from an image that has stayed with me for a while now. I return to this image throughout the book; it forms the shape of what is written. Sometimes, trauma is talked of as an overwhelming experience, of having your very being torn apart, of being torn into pieces. This is where we begin in Chapter 1, with exploring trauma and the agony of this ripping. The chapter sets the scene by charting the impact of trauma: what it feels like in the body, how it shapes our emotions and how it lingers long after the event. This chapter also starts to name the added complexity when abuse happens in faith spaces, where spiritual language and power are used to cause deep harm. It's not always easy reading, but it gives us a shared grounding for what follows.

Chapter 2 looks at why we so often end up blaming victims, even when we don't mean to. It explores how trauma messes with our thinking; and how both victims and those around them try to make sense of something that feels senseless. Our brains lean on ideas such as 'bad things happen to bad people' to protect us from fear; these, however, can lead to unfair assumptions and painful misunderstandings. Drawing on cognitive psychology, the chapter unpacks myths such as the belief in a just world, attribution error and hindsight bias: all of which can distort empathy and perpetuate blame. The story of Job is used to challenge these ideas, showing how blame is often wrongly placed on those who are suffering, and to suggest that existential rage against God can become the site of divine encounter.

Chapter 3 explores how purity culture and rape culture intersect, particularly within Christian communities, and how Scripture can be misused to uphold both. It begins by re-reading the story in John 8, often referred to as 'the woman caught in adultery', to reveal how religious power and shame can be weaponized against victims. The chapter then traces how purity teachings contribute to silencing survivors, reinforcing shame and protecting perpetrators. It calls for a more faithful, trauma-informed response from the Church: one that names sexual violence clearly, supports survivors, and interprets Scripture with integrity and care.

Survivors of abuse, especially those who challenge a church's image of purity or cohesion, may find themselves subtly or overtly silenced and excluded. Chapter 4 explores the deep and sometimes hidden dynamics of scapegoating, within church communities, in response to disclosures of sexual violence. Drawing from its biblical origins in Leviticus and psychological theory, the chapter traces how the ancient ritual of the scapegoat (meant to cleanse a community symbolically) continues in modern forms, often targeting the most vulnerable, pushing survivors into a modern-day wilderness. The chapter ends by returning to the story of the woman accused in John 8. Here, Jesus offers a radical alternative: he disrupts scapegoating by standing in solidarity with the victim, restoring her dignity and inviting us to do the same.

Chapter 5 goes on to explore what happens when survivors of sexual violence turn to the criminal justice system. Drawing on national data, case studies and personal experience, it traces the

INTRODUCTION

steep decline from the number of assaults that occur to the tiny fraction that result in conviction. It asks why so few survivors report to the police, what makes the process so slow and often retraumatizing for those who do, and why so few cases reach trial or end in conviction. Alongside this, it considers what survivors are left with when justice is delayed, denied or simply not possible. While acknowledging that the system can work (and I share a rare example where it has), it's clear that such outcomes are the exception, not the norm.

Chapter 6, 'Perfect Victims', explores the pressure placed on survivors to be flawless. Moving from the courtroom, where survivors must be the perfect victim, to the Cross, where Jesus is proclaimed as the perfect sacrifice, I explore how survivors can navigate these concepts and beliefs. By examining how Christians have come to understand the violence of the Cross, theories of atonement are considered through the lens of survivors' experience; calling for a more spacious and compassionate theology of atonement, which resists glorifying pain and recognizes Christ's solidarity with the oppressed and abused.

Confession and absolution are examined in Chapter 7, which explores how easily these familiar parts of worship can cause harm when we're not paying attention to the language we use. It looks at the difference between guilt and shame: that guilt is connected to actions committed, while shame often clings to who we are. For many survivors, feelings of shame come not from sin they've committed, but from what they've suffered. And yet, in worship, shame and sin are often spoken about as if they're the same thing. This chapter invites us to notice the damage that we can do and to consider how we might create more spacious, compassionate practices: ones that reflect the Jesus we see in the Gospels – challenging the powerful and drawing close to those who carry wounds.

Chapter 8 explores the complexity of forgiveness in the aftermath of trauma and violence. It challenges simplistic theological narratives and examines the damaging ways forgiveness has at times been misused by churches to silence victims or deflect justice. Drawing on the work of Stephen Cherry (2024) and

Marian Partington (2012), the chapter holds space for slowness, anger and contradictions that often accompany the process. Rather than offering neat answers, the chapter wrestles with forgiveness as a deeply personal, sometimes holy, sometimes impossible, response to harm. It explores the possibility that forgiveness, if it comes at all, may arise not from the duty to forgive, but from truth-telling and embodied care.

Chapter 9 explores what recovery could look like, drawing on the wisdom of survivors who know that courtroom verdicts rarely bring healing. Justice, they remind us, isn't primarily about punishment but about truth, accountability and repair. For the church, that means much more than writing safeguarding policies: it's about listening without defensiveness; naming harm honestly; resisting victim blaming; and choosing solidarity that lasts beyond the crisis moment. This chapter looks at how communities of faith can begin to embody that costly work of repair: creating safer cultures; supporting survivors on their terms; challenging damaging theologies; and taking responsibility not only with words but with actions.

* * *

When I started writing, I wasn't sure where it would lead. In some ways, the journalling, reflecting, speaking and writing, which have developed into these chapters, have been part of my own story of repair. The book has written me as I have tried to make sense of what happened and chart my recovery. At times, I have wondered who I am writing this for. For those harmed and trying to work through the mess? Or is it a guide for the Church on how to be better? In the end, it is something of a mix. It reflects where I am, where I stand – both as victim and priest – asking, 'How can we recover and how can we be better?'

But it is also more than that. The path to repair requires both survivors and the wider church community. The path to recovery belongs to the survivor; but the responsibility for truth and repair belongs to the Church. The Church bears responsibility for the

INTRODUCTION

harm caused and must play its part supporting recovery, standing in solidarity, and working for a safer world and fairer system of justice.

The movement from ripping to joining is not a straightforward or simple path. It is not about re-forming or patching together what was before, when so much has been lost. Rather, it holds out the hope that joining up the pieces in an altered but recognizable way is possible. We can long for a type of healing that restores things to how they were, with everything back in its right place; but often our experiences of recovery are more complicated. Where we have been torn and ripped, rejoining comes in different ways; and, although the path to recovery cannot mean going back or perfectly remaking what has been broken, the pieces can join, woven into something different and beautiful. The process of re-joining the pieces makes space for new colours, new threads, new patterns to emerge – an altered whole that carries the truth of its history without being defined only by its breaking. This is the image I see at the heart of the gospel: Christ torn and broken and bringing about a deeper joining than we could have imagined. Scattered fragments are gathered up, the pieces of our lives can be joined again, not as they once were, but in a new and living wholeness.

1

Rips and Tears

It's May and the sun is blazing; but it's hard to tell in this cold, damp church. We're sitting at the back, grouped around rickety tables, engaging in all the usual banter that accompanies the opening of a safeguarding training session. The clergyman next to me embodies the stereotype of the cheery, rotund vicar. I imagine I'm giving off all the vibes of an angsty feminist priest, but he doesn't seem to pick up on this; neither does my non-verbal communication appear to be dampening his spirit. Today, we are learning about domestic abuse. It's obligatory training; and, as we quickly find out, some people are present because they have been summoned and have had to set aside 'more important stuff' to be here. Others are interested and eager to learn. Some are refreshing their quite considerable knowledge and are keen to make sure we all know how much they know already.

Quite soon into the session, we are each given a figure of a person, cut out of white A4 printer paper. These are our paper people; we can choose their names. A scenario is read out and we're all asked to make a tear in our paper figures each time we hear something in the story that might undermine a person's confidence: each time there is an insult, action or controlling behaviour that might make an individual smaller; each thing that might decrease their power or agency; each occurrence that might reduce their ability to make good choices or limit their avenues to get help.

At first, the story highlights some odd or unfortunate things: nothing too serious, we think, as we make small tears in our paper people. The story carries on and small tears become larger, occasionally dramatic, ones. But it's the repetition of all the small tears that gets to me: they mingle together into one weighty assault on my paper person – the collective burden of a hundred seemingly insignificant events.

Soon we are all sitting behind piles of ripped-up paper. The banter and cheeriness are over for today's session. We each stare at our person, who is no longer recognizable as anything other than a heap of rips and tears. A hush dampens the atmosphere of the already dank church. No one wants to look up, so we keep staring at the ripped-up pieces. We knew where this was going at the start; but, even so, we've been shocked into feeling something we were not expecting. Only minutes before, these were just flimsy bits of paper; but they became our paper people and now they are in pieces. And we couldn't do anything to stop it.

For some in the room, the paper isn't just a pile of rips and tears. It represents individuals with real names and real lives beyond the paper. Some are looking at their person and seeing themselves or their past: she is them and they are her or have been. Others are seeing them for the first time. This seeing tugs at memories: times when they know they have chosen not to see or chosen to look away to avoid seeing altogether.

It's a surprisingly powerful exercise. Together, in a short space of time, we are pulled into the visceral impact of trauma: into the rips and tears depicting the wounds inflicted on our paper people and their overwhelming effect. There is collective shock in the room: is it guilt? Is it confusion about the emotions we feel towards these shreds of paper? The speed of breaking and the seemingly inevitable result has been chastening, silencing; we have become hapless bystanders, unsure of what we should do, what we could have done; and we are frozen in our indecision. We remind ourselves that this is just training: no people, paper or otherwise, were harmed in this exercise. We recover our composure and sit back into our training mode personas.

Trauma

The word trauma originates from the Greek word for a physical wound, a physical breaking or piercing of the flesh. Although today we talk of trauma as the emotional response to wounding, the images of physical rips and tears can help us to understand the psychological impact of trauma. A physical wound in the flesh can be seen and examined; the extent of damage assessed; and the process of healing logged. The injury and resulting scar tissue act as visible reminders. They reveal the state and stage of healing and show any long-term damage. Unlike an external wound, the internal effects of trauma are less easy to see; but these internal ruptures, the rips and tears, are no less damaging. However, their hiddenness can leave them unattended and untreated for longer, which may have a deeper and longer-lasting impact.

It's wrong to assume that traumatic events must be visible or dramatic emergencies, such as natural disasters, acts of terrorism or experiences of war. Other occurrences, such as domestic violence, slavery, child abuse and sexual assault, may be more concealed and seem quite different in nature but cause similar internal impact. Perhaps these could be described as society's hidden wounds. Chronic, lower-impact harm can also cause a trauma response, such as belittlement and bullying, spiritual abuse, race- or gender-based prejudice and hate, coercive control and neglect.

While these occurrences are very different in nature, the comparable experience is one of being overwhelmed and of being unable to control or stop what is happening. With this comes an accompanying sense of disbelief and shock, numbness and the growing realization that you have lost any sense of control. You cannot stop this; you cannot control what is happening to you. It is this loss of control that can be bewildering and overwhelming.

When faced with a natural disaster, when a random and uncontrollable force physically reorders your world, it is terrifying and unbelievable; but you can see that this overpowering force has rendered you powerless. Things that were solid and stable are literally turned to rubble. The world you knew has been ripped

THE PIECES JOIN

and torn to pieces; you must find a way to survive today and find ways to rebuild your tomorrow. Likewise, when your world is reordered by something personally overwhelming, but less obvious or physically tangible, it is difficult to make sense of what is happening or to communicate to others who cannot see it. The experience may be of an uncontrollable force fracturing your body, your world; but there may be little concrete evidence that anything has changed.

It can feel bewildering and confusing when seemingly lower-impact events accumulate slowly over time. These smaller rips and tears may cause as much internal damage as larger rips but may be harder to identify. We are psychologically primed for stranger-danger but, statistically, we are far more likely to be damaged by people or institutions whom we know, trust and love. When this happens, confusing and contradictory emotions, thoughts and beliefs make identifying abusive behaviour difficult and complicated.

Our brains and bodies respond to the trauma while we struggle to accept whether these acts could have been done by this person in this place. This can be compounded when abuse happens in religious settings. Victims may have to contend with a complicated mix of beliefs and emotions about God, about their perceived sinfulness and complicity, about their identity, and about the reality of what is happening. How do you begin to make sense out of what has happened when the very place or person you believed was safe and trustworthy has abused that trust?

Flight or fight may seem like appropriate responses to a violent or threatening situation, but freezing is as likely. Paralysis, shock and confusion occur as the brain shuts down certain areas and activates others in an attempt to survive. While freezing is a common and very normal response to assault, it can be hard to understand. Why didn't they respond or defend themselves? Why didn't they scream for help or try to get away?

Dissociation

The ripped-paper-person exercise demonstrates the effect of ongoing aggressions and the overwhelming impact this can have over time. The language of ripping and tearing can also be helpful as an image. This is how some people describe their experiences of trauma: as being torn into pieces or even as being torn away from one's own self. It is this rupture, this ripping or tearing, reducing normality to powerlessness, which is felt in tangible and yet hard to describe ways.

Being ripped away from yourself can feel like being disconnected from yourself and the world around you. It can seem as if your mind is temporarily disconnecting from what's happening or that you're zoning out. It can feel as if the world around you is unreal. You seem to lose track of time; you discover gaps in your memory, when you're unsure of what happened or where you were. It can feel as if you're not really there at all. It can feel as though you're outside your body, looking down at yourself, seeing where you are, and what is happening around you. It can feel like pressing a pause button on your mind.

This ripping and tearing is sometimes referred to as dissociation: a cognitive process in which a person disconnects from their thoughts and feelings, from their memories or even from their own sense of identity. Although experiences of dissociation can be quite different, this is the mind's way of coping with what is happening; the mind's way of defending itself and surviving in the presence of a perceived overwhelming threat. In that moment, the brain acts for survival, enabling this short-term, protective blocking mechanism.

After-effects

This survival mechanism, which has evolved as a protective response to threat, results in short- and longer-term effects. Early physical reactions to trauma can include exhaustion, confusion, sadness and anxiety. In the confusion, the brain tries to respond.

THE PIECES JOIN

It replays the events, looking for solutions and meaning. It rehearses what happened and actively processes other options or choices as it tries to work out how to stay safe in future. These can play on a seemingly never-ending loop, as no configuration brings the resolution the mind is looking for. Flashbacks, insomnia, headaches and nausea can be symptoms of this continuous replay. The mind tries to sort through the mess of memories, responding to recollections with heightened emotions. These memories can be triggered by similar incidents and, confusingly, by seemingly unrelated sounds, sights and smells, causing unpredictable reactions as the brain tries to keep itself safe.

Panic attacks, flashbacks, nightmares and anxiety can make sleep difficult. The continuing lack of sleep has a knock-on effect on an individual's ability to function and increases the impact of other physical and mental symptoms. Victims may use drugs and alcohol to numb their feelings, which further affects their ability to function and can leave them in dangerous and vulnerable situations; it may also lead to drug and alcohol dependency.

Victims can feel intense shame and often blame themselves for what happened. They can feel hopeless and powerless. They can also be left feeling detached, depressed or irate. These emotions may suddenly appear and seem uncontrollable. Trauma, especially when left unacknowledged or unsupported, can sometimes lead people to project their pain on to others. Survivors may carry deep wounds of shame, fear or anger; and, without safe spaces for recovery, those emotions can surface in harmful ways. In some cases, people who have been hurt may, consciously or unconsciously, repeat patterns of harm as a way of regaining control or avoiding vulnerability.

Anxiety and numbness can lead to withdrawal, affecting the ability to work, to access support or to maintain friendships. When sexual violence has occurred, victims can be left to deal with STIs, pregnancy, abortion and other sexual-health issues. The social stigma associated with sexual abuse and rape can intensify emotions and increase a sense of alienation.

These different impacts combine and affect one another; and experienced all together, they often seem overwhelming. The combined effect of physical, mental and emotional damage can develop into longer-term problems and have a lasting impact on health and well-being, even when the person appears to be coping well with what they have been through.

The body remembers

One of the most well-known ideas in trauma research is summed up in the title of Bessel van der Kolk's book *The Body Keeps the Score* (2015). It's become a kind of shorthand for something many people instinctively know but haven't always had the words for. Trauma does not simply live in our memories or in the stories we tell. It often lodges itself in the body: in the way we breathe, in the tension we carry, in the places where our body aches or falls silent. For many survivors, trauma is not something they remember so much as something they feel: a tightening in the chest; a shrinking away from touch; a sense of alertness that never quite settles.

This may feel shameful, but it is not about weakness or failure. These embodied responses are part of how the body tries to keep us safe. When something deeply frightening or violating happens, especially when it happens repeatedly or within relationships that were supposed to be safe, the nervous system adapts. It might move into fight or flight mode, or it might shut down altogether. These responses are not chosen: they are automatic. They are the body's attempt to protect itself when words, logic or control are no longer possible.

Over time, though, these protective strategies can become patterns. We might find ourselves hyper-aware of danger, flinching from sounds, unable to relax. Or we might feel numb, disconnected from ourselves or lost in shame. The body can hold on to trauma long after the mind has tried to move on. Survivors often describe this as feeling stuck: caught in responses that seem out of proportion, but which are rooted in very real experiences of harm.

Practitioners and researchers from a range of backgrounds have explored this embodied nature of trauma. Somatic therapists, such as Peter Levine (1997) and Pat Ogden and others (2006), describe how trauma can be stored in the muscles, breath and posture; and how healing can begin not just through words, but also through gentle, bodily awareness and movement. Others, such as Stephen Porges (Porges and Porges, 2023), have helped us to understand how the nervous system responds to threat, and how safety and connection can help to re-regulate the body's sense of what is possible.

Gabor Maté (Maté and Maté, 2022) shows how trauma and stress play out in our physical health, not just as symptoms but also as part of the way the body tries to adapt and survive. He writes about how the body can carry unspoken pain and how early trauma, especially when it goes unrecognized, can shape everything: from our emotional lives to our immune systems.

Joy DeGruy's research (2005) shows how the impact of slavery trauma can affect multiple generations. She also outlines the extent of the widespread and continued effects of living with this trauma in racially hostile environments.

Of course, not all survivors experience trauma in the same way; but for many, especially those who have been harmed in relationships or communities of trust, the impact is deeply physical. This is important to acknowledge, especially in faith settings where trauma has sometimes been treated only as a spiritual issue or where survivors have been urged to 'forgive and move on', without space for the complex, embodied work of recovery.

Spiritual abuse strikes at the very heart of a person's identity, often cloaked in the language of God, love or obedience. When trust in a religious leader or community is betrayed, the resulting trauma can be profound, leading to post-traumatic stress symptoms or complex PTSD (post-traumatic stress disorder). Unlike single-event trauma, spiritual abuse can be chronic, cumulative, and entangled with one's core sense of self, belonging and meaning. The damage can seem existential if victims feel cut off from the very spiritual resources that might have once brought comfort and peace.

Hilary McBride (2021) explores how religious trauma often leaves scars not only in our beliefs but also deep within our bodies. For survivors of spiritually abusive environments, the body can become a site of memory and resistance, holding the weight of fear, hypervigilance and disconnection. Some religious cultures can emphasize the body as the problem: contaminated with sin and fear or as the site of temptation. However, recovery is supported when the body is not seen as a problem to be overcome but as a profound place of healing and theological truth. In a church culture that has too often privileged doctrine over embodiment, there is a pressing need to reclaim a theology that honours the body as sacred. Here, we encounter the divine not through disembodied ideas, but in breath, sensation and the slow work of recovering a sense of safety.

Longer-term effects

Children who have lived through adverse traumatic experiences have increased chances of developing seemingly unrelated physical symptoms and chronic diseases in adulthood, such as heart disease, cancer and diabetes. These are thought to be brought on by the damage and stress the body has experienced. Survivors of rape and childhood sexual abuse are at a higher risk of developing mental-health problems, such as depression, anxiety and PTSD. These mental-health issues can have a significant impact on an individual's daily life, relationships and overall well-being; and they can sometimes develop into serious psychological disorders.

Survivors may struggle with ongoing low self-esteem and feelings of shame and guilt. They may blame themselves for the abuse and feel that they are unworthy or unlovable. Victims of rape and childhood sexual abuse may struggle with trusting others, especially in intimate relationships. They may also have difficulty forming and maintaining healthy relationships. Survivors who struggle to trust others may become isolated, less able to access friendship, help or professional support.

Survivors may experience sexual problems, such as difficulty with arousal, pain during sex and sexual dysfunction. Children who experience sexual abuse may grow up with a distorted view of sexuality and gender roles, making them more vulnerable to sexual violence as adults.

It is important to recognize that not all victims of rape and childhood sexual abuse will experience long-term psychological or emotional effects. Everyone's response to trauma is unique and influenced by a variety of factors, including personal resilience, how they come to understand the trauma, the meaning it plays in their life, and the resources and support systems they can access. However, for those who do struggle with the lasting impacts of anxiety, depression, PTSD or difficulties in relationships, seeking professional help can be a crucial step in their recovery. Mental-health professionals, including therapists, counsellors and support groups, can provide survivors with a safe space to process their experiences, develop coping strategies and work towards reclaiming their sense of self and well-being. Interventions, such as trauma-focused therapy, cognitive behavioural therapy (CBT) or eye movement desensitization and reprocessing (EMDR), can be particularly effective in helping survivors heal, regain control over their lives and cultivate a greater sense of hope for the future.

For some survivors, their journey of recovery leads them to support others who have endured similar experiences. Becoming an advocate, mentor or peer supporter can provide a sense of purpose and empowerment, transforming pain into a means of fostering change and solidarity. Engaging in survivor-led support groups, activism or educational initiatives can be an important part of their own recovery, as it allows them to give meaning to their trauma while helping others navigate their recovery processes. By sharing their stories, offering guidance or advocating for systemic change, survivors not only contribute to a more compassionate and informed society but also find strength in community and connection.

Abuse in faith settings

Abuse in religious settings carries layers of complexity that can make it damaging in particular ways. Like other forms of abuse, it involves manipulation and the misuse of power and control. But when it happens in a faith context, it often strikes at the heart of a person's identity, beliefs and sense of meaning. It can feel like a betrayal, not just by a person or a community but also by God.

Spiritual abuse is often subtle and difficult to name. It might involve controlling behaviour disguised as pastoral care; the use of Scripture to manipulate or shame; or a culture where questioning leadership is seen as disobedience or lack of faith. Spiritual abuse causes emotional and psychological harm; and it can also include aspects of financial, physical and sexual abuse.

What makes this so damaging is that faith for many people is deeply personal and profoundly shaping. It's not just what they believe: it's how they make sense of the world; how they understand right and wrong, who they are and how they relate to others. So, when abuse happens in a faith setting, especially when it's cloaked in religious language, the harm often touches the very core of a person's being.

One of the added dimensions is the way abusers may present themselves as speaking for God. When someone says, 'This is what God wants', 'You're going against Scripture' or 'You must submit to leadership', it can be incredibly difficult to push back, especially if the person hearing it has been raised in a tradition that values obedience, submission or deference to authority. Victims may be left confused, ashamed and unsure whether they're experiencing abuse or simply failing spiritually.

Religious communities can also become places where secrecy and silence are encouraged, either directly or indirectly. There may be strong messages about forgiveness, unity or not damaging the Church's reputation, which make it hard to speak out. Victims may fear that they won't be believed or, worse, that they'll be blamed for what happened. Many have been told that they're being divisive, unfaithful or unforgiving if they try to name their experience or seek justice.

For some survivors, the Church has been their spiritual home: the place they've gone to for comfort, hope and belonging. Some talk of the church as being their family, their community. To experience abuse in that space is to feel as if the ground has been pulled from underneath them. They may struggle with prayer and worship because those things are now tied up with memories of pain and betrayal. They may feel spiritually homeless and isolated from their community, their friends and their family.

While many survivors find support outside the Church and some choose to leave, others long to hold on to their faith, even while grieving what has been lost. That can be a very lonely road. Often, church support is offered only if survivors stay quiet or forgive quickly. Some survivors are told their suffering is a test of faith or that it's part of God's mysterious plan. These responses don't just fail to support the person: they deepen the harm.

Spiritual abuse is harmful in what it twists: it distorts trust, love and grace. It takes sacred language and uses it to manipulate and harm. For recovery to happen, survivors need space to speak about what happened without pressure to protect the institution or tidy up the pain. They need to be able to ask difficult theological questions about God, about suffering, about justice and forgiveness, without being silenced or rushed to resolution. For those who still hold on to faith, part of the recovery may involve finding new language for God, new ways of worshipping, or new communities where safety and honesty are truly honoured.

Paths to recovery

This chapter has offered a broad overview of how abuse and trauma can have an impact on individuals: emotionally, physically, mentally and spiritually. It names some of the visible and hidden wounds; it also identifies the long-reaching effects of harm that might show up months, even years, later. But while shared patterns and common effects can help us to recognize and understand trauma, they never capture the whole story. Abuse is not experienced in the same way by everyone. Each person carries their own unique history, personality, relationships, coping mechanisms and support networks. These things shape the impact of trauma and how it is lived with and lived through. There is no single script for how someone responds and no single linear recovery path. People find different ways of describing their experiences and themselves. Some prefer to use the term 'survivor', which acknowledges that they have come through something and are still here. It places the emphasis not on what was done to them, but on their strength and endurance: their refusal to be defined by the harm. Others choose to identify as victims. For them, this word acknowledges the truth: that something terrible happened to them, which was not their fault; that they were hurt by someone else; that they could not stop it.

Others feel uneasy with both 'victim' and 'survivor'. The words don't really capture what happened; neither seems to be connected to their experience. Perhaps the words feel too loaded, too associated with narratives in which they don't recognize themselves. They may simply not want to use any label at all. Naming can be powerful; but so is the right to choose when, how or whether to name what has happened.

What matters most is that people are given space to speak with their own voices. To describe what they have lived through and how they now see themselves; to give words to what may have been long unspoken. It may be through narrative, through art, through movement or symbol. But finding a way to articulate what was once unspeakable can be a key part of recovery. It is a reclaiming of story, of identity, of voice.

In this book, I use the terms 'survivor' and 'victim' interchangeably. They are the most widely recognized and commonly used in professional and support contexts; and they help to signal the subject matter clearly. But I am mindful that these words may not resonate with everyone; there are many other ways to name experience.

This book focuses on abuse that takes place in Christian contexts and explores some of the pastoral and theological implications of that abuse. Its lens is deliberately angled towards faith settings, particularly churches, and the unique complexities that can arise in these spaces. Abuse within these contexts is often shaped by particular dynamics of trust, forgiveness, power, authority and belief. These dynamics can deeply influence how abuse is experienced; how it is disclosed or silenced; and how it is responded to by those within the Church.

Because of this focus, this book is not a comprehensive guide to recovery; nor does it aim to replace the role of professional psychological care. It doesn't explore in detail the different forms of professional talking therapy that can support survivors while processing their trauma and rebuilding their lives. But it is important to say clearly here how vital these services are.

Professional therapy offers something this book cannot: a personalized, clinically informed space to explore trauma with someone trained to understand the brain, the body and the road to recovery. Therapists can support survivors in navigating the aftermath of abuse through trauma-focused therapies, counselling, cognitive approaches and other specialist interventions. These spaces can offer containment, safety and insight, and provide an anchor in what might otherwise feel like a shapeless and endless process.

For many survivors, professional support is not simply helpful: it is essential. It can make the difference between being stuck and beginning to move again; between being overwhelmed and finding a way to breathe. No one should have to face the consequences of abuse alone. Churches and communities can play a vital part in surrounding survivors with care and solidarity. But they are not substitutes for therapy: they cannot provide what trained professionals can. Where access is possible, professional support should always be encouraged.

What this book does try to offer, however, is a theological and pastoral response to the particular challenges that come with being a survivor within the Christian faith. For those who choose to stay within the Church or continue to engage with Christian belief, there are often painful and complex hurdles to navigate. How do you trust again in a context where trust was shattered? How do you pray, sing hymns or open a Bible when the same language or liturgy was used to justify harm; or when the person who hurt you stands at the front in a clerical collar or robes? How do you untangle your image of God from the actions of those who claimed to represent God?

These are not small questions and they don't have easy answers. Some victims make the difficult and understandable decision to step away from church altogether. Others find their faith reshaped, broken or renewed in unexpected ways. Some walk away from formal religion but still hold on to a spiritual sense of connection. Others find new expressions of faith outside the walls where harm occurred. All these responses are valid. This book does not prescribe a path but seeks to hold space for the many ways survivors journey with, or away from, faith.

Trauma lodges itself deep within us; not just in our memories but in our breath, our heartbeat, our instincts. It's in the way our bodies flinch before we think, in the weight we carry in our shoulders, in the breath we hold. Sometimes, our bodies remember things long after our minds try to forget. Recognizing trauma as something held in the body is not to medicalize it or reduce it to biology. It is, rather, to honour the fullness of who we are – body, mind, and spirit – and to recognize that recovery must attend to all these dimensions. In time, and with the right kind of support, the body can begin to feel safe again. It may be slow; it may require gentleness and care. Even so, the pieces that were ripped can join again: not seamlessly or perfectly; but rebuilding is possible.

2

Who Is to Blame?

Victims and survivors can be left with weighty questions and self-accusations.

Could I have stopped it?
Should I have known what to do?
Is this my fault?
Did I bring this on myself?
Do I deserve it?

We may be tempted to think these questions should be easy to answer. After all, a victim of a crime is just that, a victim, and so not to blame. But experience suggests otherwise. Victims replay events and scenarios as the mind tries to process and comprehend what has happened. By doing this, the brain is trying to unravel an unimaginable event; to put words to something unspeakable; to make sense of something senseless. If we take the image of trauma as an experience of ripping or tearing, the brain is trying to fathom this unexpected rupture: to untangle what has been torn to shreds; to try to pull the pieces back together.

The cognitive effects of trauma, such as memory lapse and ruptures in the timeline, further complicate matters. The brain tries to sort through the confusion by replaying events over and over again – looking for order, looking for reasons. If the brain can make sense of this, if it can make sense of why it happened, it might be able to stop it from happening again. These recurring remembrances can happen consciously, with memories and intrusive thoughts occupying wakeful hours, or subconsciously, disrupting sleep and causing nightmares. Returning again and

WHO IS TO BLAME?

again to these types of questions in an attempt to sort through the confusion is very normal, irrespective of the circumstances of what actually happened.

Alongside this self-questioning, victims are affected by how other people respond. Friends, family and colleagues may wish to be supportive but can be shocked or unsure of what to say. They may find the events overwhelming and simply not know what to do. They may feel traumatized, as well, and not want to believe or accept that it has happened. Victims can be left wondering why friends and family are treating them in this way.

Why don't they believe me?
Why are they questioning me?
Why can't they look me in the eye?
Why are they avoiding me?
Why are they treating me like this?
Why are they blaming me?

Many victims experience memory loss or confusion. While these are common symptoms, it can be hard for others to understand why they can't remember what happened; why the account seems to change; or why extra details are added later. This can make conversations tough; it may seem preferable to shut down the conversation rather than work through difficult things, especially if the conversation is upsetting everyone.

When victims ask for support from those around them but are met instead with a confusing or negative response, it can be extremely damaging. Sadly, research findings consistently show that we tend to blame victims rather than support them and believe them. We might want to assume that we would be supportive when someone discloses a traumatic experience; but evidence suggests that a much more normal human response is to blame and ostracize victims. In fact, some of the ways our brains are wired actually contribute to this, emphasizing incorrect myths about victims, rather than assessing events without bias.

Myth 1: Bad things happen to bad people

The ways in which our brains have evolved to process threat and our need to feel safe skew our perceptions and our empathy towards victims. When we hear about traumatic experiences, we don't just respond to the person in front of us and to what they are saying, but also to our body's own reaction to keep itself safe.

We are shaped by a view of the world sometimes referred to as *just world theory* (Lerner, 1980). This is the belief that good things happen to good people and, conversely, bad things happen to bad people. In many ways, this type of thinking is helpful. It evolved as one of our cognitive processes, helping us to moderate our behaviour and to live within a moral code. A belief in a just and ordered world encourages us to strive to be good, to be fair, to be truthful: arguably, all things that are necessary for a good society. If good things happen to good people, then it is worth putting in the effort to be good; and, if more effort is put into being good, the chances are that you will benefit from this. But this also skews our view of victims because if we believe that good things happen to good people and bad things happen to bad people, then victims must in some way be responsible for their misfortune.

This type of thinking helps to protect our mental health by giving us the illusion that we can keep ourselves safe from harm. To live in a world of random violence, where we may at any point be under threat, is too much for our minds to hold together. How could we cope with living in a world in which we could come under attack at any moment – and under attack from those we love and trust most? While this is arguably a more accurate and realistic view of the world, how could we thrive living with that knowledge? Would we be able to move beyond the paralysing anxiety of it?

One way in which our cognitive processes have developed to protect us from crippling anxiety is by holding on to the belief that the world is a just and fair place, and that our lives are ordered. We can learn to navigate a violent world if it is also an ordered world: a world that is just and fair; a world where there

WHO IS TO BLAME?

are rules. We can learn to negotiate a violent but ordered world by acting responsibly and believing that if we do the *right* things and believe the *right* things, we will have good lives and avoid or minimize harm. This helps us to steer through what we see all around us; it helps us to keep living in a trusting and open way, believing that if we are good, good things will happen to us.

But this way of thinking is also highly problematic and has trained our minds to assume that negative experiences are the result of bad or questionable behaviour. To protect our view of the world, we make assumptions and hold on to the belief that we are good people, who do good things and therefore will experience good results. To believe we live in a world in which random violent things happen to innocent victims is too threatening a world to live and thrive in. This would be a world in which, at any point, we could be attacked, or lose our possessions, our loved ones or even ourselves. To counter this level of anxiety, we buy into these binary beliefs about good and bad people, though we may not be conscious of doing so. These beliefs skew how we perceive victims, allowing us more readily to apportion blame to them. If they are in some way responsible, this keeps the threat at arm's length. We tell ourselves we are good, we act in positive and appropriate ways, so we are not in danger. After all, bad things happen to bad people.

So, when we see someone in trouble, someone just like us, someone whom we would have previously judged as *good*, our beliefs clash and we have a choice. Do we minimize, reducing the experience to something not all that serious? Or do we even deny that it happened because bad things don't really happen to good people? Or do we accept that a bad thing has happened, retaining our belief that bad things happen to bad people, and so look for ways the victim has contributed to what happened? Or do we allow our beliefs to be challenged and accept that bad things happen to good people, however frightening that might be?

We have the option to change our assumptions and accept that random and calamitous events do indeed happen to good people, people just like us, but this may be too challenging to accept. To protect ourselves from this level of threat and anxiety, our minds have learnt to twist what we perceive and we are barely conscious of it. By blaming the victim, we can retain the illusion that such terrible things do not happen to good people and so could not happen to us.

In Christian settings, these beliefs can be compounded through an appeal to Scripture. The blessings promised for obedience to God and curses as punishment for disobedience, which are listed in Deuteronomy, appear to mirror the binary thinking that good things happen to good people and bad things happen to bad people. Prosperity theologies develop this idea, encouraging the belief that health and wealth are signs of divine favour. However, this is firmly challenged in the many Gospel stories and teachings of Jesus; and in the story of Job, which we'll return to later in the chapter.

Myth 2: It must be their fault

Another way in which our brains are wired to blame rather than support victims is through our tendency to attribute cause and blame in a biased way. This is sometimes referred to as attribution error (Ross, 1977). When something negative happens to us, we are more likely to look for an external reason for the situation: to look for someone else, or something else, to blame. However, if someone else experiences something bad or fails in some way, we are more likely to attribute this to them, believing that this negative experience is linked to them: to something they did or to something they are. The effect of this is that we generally tend to hold others unreasonably responsible for their misfortune, which differs from how we judge ourselves.

When abuse or assault happens to others, we may unconsciously look to identify how their attributes or actions may have contributed to what happened. This may help us to feel safer and less anxious, as we can convince ourselves that we do not have the (weak, foolish or morally questionable) attributes the victim has. After all, we would not dress like that, trust that person, get drunk, walk home alone, or whatever act or choice we mark as contributing to the harm. However, when we think like this, our perception is based more on our attribution bias than the specifics of what actually happened.

Myth 3: They should have known better

Humans have the tendency to process events with hindsight bias, believing that it's possible to predict events and adapt our behaviour accordingly. Hindsight is a really useful tool, giving us the ability to reflect on past events; but it can also reduce the empathy we feel towards victims. We use hindsight after events have happened to identify the causes; and, in doing so, we hope to learn alternative ways to act in future. However, this can lead to hindsight bias, from which we unconsciously assume that the learning that happens after an event (hindsight learning) is available to us before events happen. This leads to the tendency to assume that victims should have realized what was about to unfold (Janoff-Bulman and Timko, 1985). If we assume that victims could have predicted what was about to happen, it can then seem reasonable to assume that they could (or *should*) have made better choices; and these better choices could have prevented or limited the damage inflicted. When we hear of a tragedy, it is a common response to ask these types of hindsight questions:

'Why didn't they realize that would happen?'
'Why did they go there?'
'Why didn't they do x, y, z, *instead?'*

Asking questions such as these is our brain's hindsight reaction; it has more to do with our evolved response to unexpected events than the circumstances of what happened. But by doing this, we begin to attribute blame to the victim for not acting with the benefit of hindsight. Of course, the benefit of hindsight comes only after the event, not before; rationally, we know this and yet our hindsight bias skews our perception. It is much more realistic to accept that the victim could not have foretold events nor acted differently; but the presence of hindsight bias in our processing pushes us away from assuming this.

Countering hindsight bias can be difficult for victims as they process what has happened. It is common for victims to blame themselves for not acting differently, for not foreseeing what would happen, or for not putting in protective or preventative measures beforehand. Friends and family, horrified by what has happened, are also likely to be engaging in hindsight questioning. How they verbalize this can either reinforce victim blaming or help to counter it by supporting the victim to accept that they were not to blame and could not have known beforehand how events might unfold.

Victim blaming in the story of Job

The Book of Job stands as one of the Bible's most raw and unsettling texts: a holy protest lodged in the heart of the Bible. Job, stripped of everything, sits in dust, his life ripped to shreds. He dares to ask the question we all carry in suffering: 'Why?' But this is not the why of neat theology or moral cause-and-effect. It is the guttural cry of a man who has done nothing to deserve what has befallen him. In Job's voice, we hear not only ancient lament but also the echo of anyone who has stood at the brink of meaningless suffering and screamed into the void.

One of the central errors explored in this ancient drama is the deep and damaging impulse to blame the victim. The book is set up to be read like a theatrical play; a moral story to teach a theological point, complete with heavenly wagers, philosophical debates and emotional monologues, all orbiting the problem of suffering and how blame is apportioned. In this context, God is seen as the force of nature, the power behind the movement of the earth, wind and sea; the power behind light and dark, day and night. Here, there is no question about whether God is behind unfolding events; rather, the question this story attends to is whether the innocent suffer. Do bad things happen only to bad people?

WHO IS TO BLAME?

Job is introduced as a moral ideal, a perfect victim, blameless in his conduct. And yet he is struck by sudden and devastating loss. In response, his friends assume a posture that is all too familiar: they suggest that Job must, in some way, be responsible for his fate. After all, they argue, good things happen to good people and bad things happen to bad people.

> Think now, who that was innocent ever perished?
> Or where were the upright cut off?
> As I have seen, those who plough iniquity
> and sow trouble reap the same.
> (Job 4.7–8)

'Repent,' they urge him. 'Confess.'

What is noticeably painful for Job, alongside the unbearable losses, is the betrayal of his friends and their inability to sit with his pain. Those he turned to for comfort turn on him: they question, moralize, doubt his integrity. He becomes not only a sufferer but a suspect. They try to convince him that he must have sinned in some way against God for this level of calamity to arise; they offer repentance as the only solution or way out. Though innocent, Job is blamed, shunned and ostracized. Job confronts his friends, attesting, with unflinching honesty, to his innocence; arguing that calamity falls on both the guilty and the innocent, and that God protects neither. And yet, in all he is experiencing, Job understands that his friends have misunderstood God. He will not be gaslit into believing that this calamity is God's punishment for his sin.

> Though I am innocent, my own mouth would condemn me;
> though I am blameless, he would prove me perverse.
> I am blameless; I do not know myself;
> I loathe my life.
> It is all one; therefore I say,
> he destroys both the blameless and the wicked.
> (Job 9.20–22)

For Job, and for many who experience trauma, victim blaming is a double bind. It layers pain upon pain. Not only must the sufferer grieve their loss and face a world suddenly emptied of meaning, but they must also carry the weight of suspicion, isolation and shame. The support systems that should have held them instead turn away.

Herman describes how survivors of trauma live with a rage that arises when the world refuses to name what has happened.

> During the process of mourning, the survivor must come to terms with the impossibility of getting even. As she vents her rage in safety, her helpless fury gradually changes into a more powerful and satisfying form of anger: righteous indignation. (Herman, 2015, p. 190)

This anger is not only understandable; it is also a rightful expression of the survivor's need for justice and recognition. As the story develops, Job gives up on trying to convince his friends that he is innocent, and turns to rage at God and to rage about God.

> Even when I cry out, 'Violence!' I am not answered;
>   I call aloud, but there is no justice.
> He has walled up my way so that I cannot pass,
>   and he has set darkness upon my paths.
> He has stripped my glory from me,
>   and taken the crown from my head.
> He breaks me down on every side, and I am gone,
>   he has uprooted my hope like a tree.
> (Job 19.7–10)

Job's speeches are the articulation of this type of existential rage; a refusal to be gaslit by a system that claims he must have deserved this. He stands before his friends, his God, and the vast silence of the cosmos and demands to be heard. There is something profoundly theological about this insistence. It is a refusal to accept the theology of suffering as something deserved. A resistance to the idea that calamity has moral justification to it. Job exposes the random cruelty of life. He names what some dare not say: that terrible things happen and there is no reason. God's response, when it finally comes, is not a justification and not an answer or an explanation to make sense of what has happened. Instead, God rages back, speaking through an almighty storm. There is something deeply uncomfortable about the divine speech Job encounters in the whirlwind. God does not defend divine justice, nor apologize. Instead, God rages too. God argues the vastness of creation and the wildness of life: all held in a mystery beyond human comprehension. In the vast mechanics of the universe, Job is small, helpless and powerless. And yet, strangely, this encounter enables transformation. Job moves from demanding an explanation, not because his pain is dismissed or the calamity resolved, but because he has been heard and seen, and has met with God.

There is something deeply holy about rage that refuses to let go of God, even as it cries out against God. Perhaps it is in this place, the place of unresolved pain and rage, that the real encounter occurs. Job stands mute before the emptiness of evil, feeling the insufficiency of any known system of explanation, and asks why. Job does not get his answers, but he gets God. And that is not nothing.

To stand and rage in the face of evil and suffering, as Job does and as many trauma survivors do, is to refuse simple theologies. It is to hold pain and presence, rage and reverence in the same breath. It is to allow space for raging lament, not as the opposite of faith but as its deepest form. And perhaps this is what the raging whirlwind offers: not justice, not clarity, but connection.

In this chapter, we have explored how our brains and our thought processes might cause us to misjudge victims, incorrectly blaming them for what happened. This pattern of victim-blaming behaviours can be traced back to the oldest texts of the Bible, as well as seen in our modern-day interactions. Chapter 3 develops these ideas by considering how religious and cultural beliefs contribute to victim blaming.

3

Toxic Myths

In John 8, we read the story of Jesus and a woman; we don't know her name. The religious leaders allege she has been caught in adultery; they demand that Jesus complies with the law and joins the crowd intent on stoning her to death. It's a story often referred to as 'The Adulterous Woman' or 'The Woman Caught in Adultery'; either title seems odd to use as there is scant evidence for the crime and so much more is going on in the story that deserves to make the headline.

Even though the accusers are opposed by Jesus, and even though no credible evidence is given, 2,000 years later we are still buying into this perception of her: that she is guilty. How we label things deeply affects our ongoing perception of them. We've seen this in the way children caught up in grooming gangs have often been referred to as child prostitutes. We see it in the news stories which distort the facts by offering headlines that shift blame on to victims, with images or words that suggest they were complicit or asking for it. We read it in the headlines that minimize the harm caused, romanticize rape or project positive values on to perpetrators.

What if the story had been given the title, 'The Wrongly Accused Woman' or 'The Woman Slut-Shamed'? What if we shifted the focus, as Jesus does in the story, and called it 'Standing Up to Abusive Religious Leaders' (O'Day, 2015, p. 535)? I wonder how that might change our perception. What if we read this narrative not through the misleading depiction of this woman, but by attending to the text and imagining what happened? So, let's start again, reading it without the misleading headline.

The religious leaders and teachers of the law drag a woman before Jesus, quoting the law – but rather selectively. She is alone. The man involved is missing. The law they cite requires evidence and witnesses; and if adultery were proven, both parties would face the same punishment. The teachers of the law would have known this and known that she alone was not enough evidence; yet they parade her before Jesus and the crowd. The text implies that this woman has been taken against her will and is being used to set a trap for Jesus. This isn't about upholding justice: it's a staged act of cruelty. Under the guise of legal righteousness, they are manipulating the situation to justify putting her to death and to corner Jesus into either condoning violence or breaking the law.

At the end of the encounter, Jesus says to the woman, 'Go your way, and from now on do not sin again' (John 8.11). It's a line that is often used to justify her condemnation: proof, some argue, that she was guilty after all; that this is a story in which Jesus shows mercy to a guilty sinner who deserved punishment. After all, he wouldn't say, 'Don't sin again,' if she hadn't been sinning. However, a similar phrase appears a little earlier in John's Gospel, when Jesus heals the man at the pool of Bethesda. After the man is healed, Jesus says, 'Do not sin any more' (John 5.14). Yet in this similar instance, we don't take this phrase as proof that it was this man's moral failure or hidden transgression that caused his disability (O'Day, 2015, p. 534).

Why are we so easily persuaded to accept the tales of the men who accuse her? Perhaps it's easier to see her as guilty and forgiven than innocent and rescued. Why do we believe what the men say about her, even though the text itself questions their motivations (John 8.6)? What if Jesus' final words to her are not proof of sin but the invitation to a life free from the entanglement of sin, free from shame, free from fear? His words, in this story, at the pool in Bethesda, and in many other Gospel accounts, seem less about verdicts and more about restoration.

Commentators have speculated about how she came to be there (O'Day, 2015, p. 532–5). Had she actually been caught in an act of adultery? Had a trap been set for her too? Was she, as some commentators argue, a victim of sexual violence? It seems much more plausible that she was a victim, making this public shaming and attempted stoning all the more horrifying.

It can be tempting to read this story and imagine this horror as something that happened in ancient cultures: something remote that would not happen today. But we need only look at how girls abused by grooming gangs have been treated by the police, by the social services, by the justice system and by society at large to see a very modern version of this story. We may think our system of law and order would not lead to the barbaric treatment of victims of sexual violence; but the treatment of girls targeted by grooming gangs is clear evidence of how this can happen today.

Honour-based abuse

Another way to understand this story in our current context is by looking at honour-based abuse. If it happened today in the UK, it would probably be recorded as an honour-based offence. The police currently log thousands of honour-based abuse (HBA) cases every year, with a significant rise in reporting rates over the past few years. While often associated with specific religious or cultural traditions, HBA is found in a range of religious and secular contexts.

HBA includes harmful behaviours committed to protect or defend the perceived honour of a family or community. It can involve coercion, violence, forced marriage or threats of shame and exclusion. It disproportionately affects women and girls, though people of all genders are targeted.

HBA can include violence or forced confinement. It might involve emotional abuse, threats or financial controls to punish and isolate the victim. Victims may be forced into marriage or experience sexual violence as a means of protecting or restoring purity. Perceived inappropriate relationships, the refusal of an arranged marriage or seeking divorce can trigger honour-based abuse. But so can dressing or behaving in ways that are deemed unacceptable or rumours and allegations of promiscuity.

Honour killings are thankfully rare and an extreme expression of shamed-based violence. However, more moderate patterns of exclusion and coercive controlling behaviour are found in a range of religious settings and may be more prevalent than commonly thought. In Christian communities, this is often wrapped in the language of purity and sexual abstinence outside marriage. Linda Kay Klein writes from an American context about the damage purity culture can cause (2018). The theologian Katie Cross writes about the problems of purity culture from a UK perspective (2020), as does Rachel Gardner, writing from the viewpoint of an evangelical youth pastor (2021). Churches may encourage particular purity practices, portraying them as being countercultural in an oversexualized society. However, Christian purity beliefs are not formed in isolation but are also underpinned and reinforced by myths and incorrect assumptions about sexual violence in the broader cultural landscape.

Rape culture

Rape culture refers to societies in which sexual violence is normalized, minimized or excused. It's not primarily about individual cases but the cultural messages we receive around sex, gender, power and consent. These messages make it more likely that sexual violence will happen; and more likely that victims won't be believed.

The #MeToo movement shone a light onto the prevalence of violence against women and girls in our society, and the inability of our policing and justice systems to address it. The protests and vigils in London in 2021, after the killing of Sarah Everard and in response to the behaviour of police officers following the murder of Bibaa Henry and Nicole Smallman, gave voice to the rage many women felt.

It is not uncommon for victims of sexual violence to be blamed. Comments about what the victim was wearing, their behaviour or whether they were drinking alcohol at the time of the assault are commonplace. Victims often face disbelief from friends, family and statutory services, which can discourage them from reporting the crime or seeking help.

The general availability of violent porn has exposed children and teens to sexual violence at levels not experienced by previous generations. The way sexual violence is portrayed in the media trivializes and sensationalizes the issue. The sexual objectification of women has become the norm and contributed to a culture where sexual violence is not taken seriously.

When society treats sexual violence as something inevitable or acceptable, it normalizes the behaviour. Phrases such as 'boys will be boys' minimize the harm caused, normalizing and excusing it. Saying things such as 'men can't control themselves' or 'it's just how things are' makes it seem as if sexual violence is a normal part of life.

The way in which high-profile cases are handled and discussed in the public sphere sends clear signals to victims. When perpetrators face little or no punishment for their actions (which may be excused as mistakes or beyond their control because they were influenced by alcohol or drugs), it reinforces the view that such behaviour is acceptable.

Many victims of sexual violence do not report due to the fears of not being believed, being blamed or being mistreated by the police. Anxiety about intrusive and combative investigations – and the fear of being ridiculed, shamed and torn apart by the court proceedings – can discourage victims from coming forward. Given the low conviction rates for rape and sexual assault in comparison to other crimes, and the lengthy amount of time it takes for those minority of cases to make it to court, victims can wonder if there is any point going through the personal cost of reporting.

There is work being done to improve the situation. Independent Sexual Violence Advisors (ISVAs) offer support services to those going through the justice system; but the coverage of services across the country is mixed. New legislation, specialist courts and survivor-informed training for police are beginning to bring change. But there is still such a long way to go.

Purity culture

Although purity culture presents itself as a counterpoint to the sexualization of wider society, its teachings can feed into rape culture in subtle and insidious ways, reinforcing shame and silencing victims under the guise of moral purity. Purity culture is a movement within Christianity that emphasizes modesty, gender roles and sexual abstinence; it links an individual's moral and spiritual worth to their sexual purity. Its teaching implies, or states outright, that if you have sex outside heterosexual marriage you are damaged goods. These messages affect everyone, but they disproportionately harm girls, women and LGBTQ+ people.

The purity movement emerged within conservative Christian communities in the US during the late twentieth century, but has had widespread influence on conservative, evangelical and charismatic Christianity within the UK. It may seem counterintuitive that beliefs shaped around women's modesty would enable a culture in which increased rates of sexual violence occur, but research on communities endorsing modesty rules show this. The irony is that communities that enforce strict modesty rules often have higher rates of sexual assault. Why? Because victims are blamed for violating purity codes and perpetrators are protected under the guise of authority, forgiveness or spiritual headship. Women and girls who are assaulted often find themselves accused of tempting men or not guarding their purity. When someone experiences sexual violence, a culture of purity beliefs may motivate church members to look unquestioningly for reasons why the victim provoked the assault.

This creates deep confusion and shame. If purity equals worth, what happens when that purity is taken from you? What does it mean for your place in the community? What does it mean for how God sees you?

While most victims of sexual violence experience shame, those in Christian communities that endorse purity culture experience intense and magnified feelings of shame and guilt when sexual violence occurs. Purity culture links sexual behaviour with moral and spiritual worth; it suggests that those who fail to remain pure are spiritually and morally tainted. This can exacerbate the trauma of sexual violence, as victims may think that their spiritual standing is also compromised by the assault.

If purity culture links an individual's moral and spiritual worth to their sexual purity, where does this leave victims of sexual violence? Will they be excluded by the community? If God hates promiscuity, does God hate them now?

Purity culture can also perpetuate myths and misinformation about sexual violence, such as the belief that it only happens to those who are promiscuous or to those who ask for it. These myths not only blame the victim but also reinforce harmful stereotypes about sexual violence. Purity culture often emphasizes external standards of behaviour and appearance, such as modesty in dress or abstaining from certain behaviours. When someone experiences sexual violence, there may be a tendency to judge the victim against these standards rather than focus on the perpetrator's actions and accountability.

In wider society, there is a tendency to silence victims. This can be exacerbated in Christian contexts influenced by purity culture and teaching. Victims may fear being judged or shamed by their community and so may choose to maintain the appearance of purity and moral integrity rather than speaking out. While this is entirely understandable, this silencing hinders survivors from seeking help and support, perpetuating the cycle of abuse and maintaining the status quo. Victims may not speak out because they fear being seen as sinful, impure or spiritually compromised. They may not speak out because they have internalized the purity teaching and believe it must be their fault. In communities where women and girls are already seen as morally responsible for men's behaviour, the pressure to remain silent is immense.

Purity culture upholds traditional gender roles, in which men are seen as leaders and women as submissive. This power dynamic creates environments where male authority and desires are prioritized over female autonomy and consent. These gender roles also make it difficult for women and girls to assert their boundaries or report sexual violence, as doing so may be seen as challenging male authority. Women and girls who do speak out can be accused of usurping male authority or of having a rebellious spirit.

Purity culture's emphasis on abstinence-only teaching often leaves individuals unprepared to navigate healthy sexual relationships or understand the complexities of consent. It creates a silence around issues of sexual violence, failing to equip people with the language or tools to recognize abuse. As a result, harmful myths about sex and consent remain unchallenged, creating conditions in which rape culture is quietly sustained.

This book focuses on sexual violence against women and girls, as this has been the context in which I have ministered. But it is important to recognize that purity culture has caused significant harm to LGBTQ+ individuals. Rape crisis centres and ISVAs recognize the particular challenges LGBTQ+ people face in accessing support and reporting assaults. These barriers are even more daunting when someone belongs to a faith community that regards queerness or same-sex relationships as sinful.

Secondary harm: how church communities respond to survivors

Victims of sexual violence in religious settings often describe the harm they experience as unfolding in multiple stages. First, there is the initial abuse itself; then a second wave of trauma follows in the response to their disclosure. Many refer to this as 're-abuse': naming the ways the Church, whether through denial, blame or silence, compounds their suffering during the reporting process. For some, the collective response of the community feels as harmful, if not more so, than the original abuse. This can sound shocking – how can a response, albeit fumbled, be labelled as abuse? How can well-intentioned pastoral care be taken in such a way? Churches need to listen to the voices of survivors and take on board what they say. Responding well to victims is an area in which a change to church culture could make a significant difference to the experience of survivors; but only if we are willing to listen and change.

Survivors of abuse within Christian communities often speak of being met not with compassion but with blame. Instead of support, they are sometimes made to feel responsible, publicly shamed or encouraged to confess, as if they were somehow at fault. Some are quietly asked to retract their disclosure, remain silent or leave the Church. Those employed by churches may find themselves facing a painful choice: to stay silent to keep their jobs, their community, their home; or to speak out and lose it all.

Others describe being drawn into formal processes of confession, where they are asked to retell what happened and to repent for their supposed part in it. Some are even encouraged to marry the person who harmed them, especially if pregnancy has occurred, under the belief that this redeems the situation. In other cases, survivors are offered prayer ministry to cleanse, purify and break soul ties. Soul ties are believed to be spiritual bonds that arise from any sexual contact, which must be severed through repentance. Survivors are asked to list the details of the abuse, confess their part in forming the soul-tie connection and seek healing through repeated prayer. If they articulate feelings of guilt or shame, which are a normal and usual response to sexual assault, they may be encouraged to confess again, to forgive the perpetrator and try harder to let go. Feelings of shame can be taken as evidence of guilt. Anger or a lack of forgiveness can be taken as a barrier to healing. And the inability to heal quickly can be explained as the individual's sinful desire to retain the soul-tie connection with the perpetrator.

These practices, often shaped by purity culture, can leave survivors with deep wounds and feeling confused, silenced and burdened by shame that was never theirs to bear. A more faithful response involves listening with care, rejecting blame, supporting victims to report sexual violence to the police, and creating communities where survivors are believed and supported. Churches should encourage survivors to seek professional therapeutic support rather than relying solely on in-house solutions and prayer ministry, which can sometimes reinforce harmful dynamics. It is essential to recognize that recovery from trauma requires expertise beyond what the Church is equipped to offer. Professional therapists, particularly those experienced in trauma-informed care, can help survivors to navigate the deep emotional and psychological effects of abuse. By supporting and validating the need for external help, the Church can show a true commitment to the well-being of its members, empowering them to recover in skilled hands.

Scripture and the reality of sexual violence

The way we teach biblical passages such as John 8, or tell the story of David and Bathsheba (2 Samuel 11) and other rape narratives (Genesis 16 and 34, 2 Samuel 13 and Judges 19—21), carries significant weight for how sexual violence is understood within the Church. When these texts are approached with sensitivity and clarity, naming sexual violence for what it is, they have the potential to counteract the damaging messages of rape culture. However, when these passages are misinterpreted, ignored or used to reinforce purity myths, they inadvertently perpetuate rape culture and further silence survivors. If John 8 is taught as the woman caught in adultery, with the focus on her assumed sin rather than the cruelty of those wrongfully accusing her, we fail both in attending to the passage and in challenging purity myths. If this story is taught without addressing the power dynamics and the trauma of victimization, it can leave survivors feeling shunned and anxious about how they will be treated if they disclose. Will they be brought out, in front of the community, to be exposed and accused of adultery? We risk similar results if the story of David and Bathsheba is taught without emphasizing the abuse of power and the exploitation involved, or if this story is simply ignored and David idolized.

We may be tempted to gloss over these difficult texts rather than name abuses. However, by doing so, we endorse unhelpful rape myths within the Church, whether or not we intend to. This may reinforce the belief that some things are unspeakable; or that those chosen by God to lead should be obeyed and revered whatever they do; or that victims are complicit or directly at fault for what happens to them.

How these passages are handled in church teaching sends a powerful, though sometimes unintended, message to victims and survivors. When we fail to confront these texts with honesty, we may inadvertently reinforce the shame and silence that keeps survivors from coming forward, while allowing harmful cultural myths to persist unchecked. Acknowledging sexual violence directly, with the pastoral and theological insight it demands, is crucial for creating a church environment where survivors are believed, supported, and empowered to seek justice and recovery.

In this chapter and the previous one, we've explored how victims of sexual violence can be blamed for what happened. This includes normal and unconscious assumptions that shape how we view the world, as well as belief systems in society and in the Church that skew our judgements. Victim blaming is painful enough on its own; but, sometimes, it doesn't stop there. Blame can escalate. What begins as victim blaming can develop into scapegoating, as communities, congregations or institutions look for someone to carry the weight of collective discomfort and shame. That's what we turn to now.

4

Scapegoat

This is too much for us to handle: you must carry it all.
What happened to you scares us; please take our fear away.

It hurts us to look at you; we don't know where to turn.
Your presence is too painful: you must leave us to our peace.

You expose the sin around us; we can't carry the burden of it.
We are dirty and defiled: you must take our shame away.

Scapegoating is a term we use, sometimes casually, when someone is unfairly blamed so others can avoid responsibility. But the reality runs deeper. While victim blaming often occurs in personal interactions, scapegoating is a collective process. It involves a group projecting its guilt, anxiety or failure on to someone else and expecting them not only to bear the blame but also to carry the shame and fear away from the community. This dynamic serves to protect the group by diverting attention from those truly responsible and directing anger or discomfort towards a convenient target. Sometimes overtly, sometimes subtly, the weight of this discomfort is placed upon the victim. They are pushed out of the community, which allows others to feel relieved, cleansed and able to carry on as though nothing had happened.

Psychologically, scapegoating functions as a kind of group defence mechanism. When something threatens the group's identity, cohesion or sense of goodness, there's an urgent need to restore balance. Blaming the person who exposes the problem is far easier than confronting the problem itself. It allows the group to preserve the illusion that it is still healthy, faithful and safe.

Social identity theory suggests that groups protect their self-image by pushing out anyone that doesn't fit their narrative (Tajfel and Turner, 1979; Girard, 1977 and 1986). Survivors, by naming abuse, don't just speak out about what happened: they expose a dark side of the group or church community. They shine a light where it's easier to keep things hidden; and in groups shaped by honour, purity or spiritual hierarchy, the impulse to preserve appearances is strong. The need to keep things looking holy can outweigh the call to do justice.

Scapegoats are often chosen because they are perceived as vulnerable or somehow different, making them easy targets for blame. This dynamic is often fuelled by unconscious bias, unequal power balance or a need to find a simple explanation for complex problems. When it comes to survivors of sexual violence, especially in church communities influenced by purity culture, this logic becomes painfully familiar. Once someone is seen as impure, as damaged or as a source of tension, scapegoating is more likely to happen. Once someone is seen in this way it becomes easier for the community to project blame on to them. The same mechanism applies to other marginalized groups in the Church: those who have less voice or power. People from other ethnicities, LGBTQ+ individuals, disabled people, children or those living in poverty – anyone perceived as different or outside the boundaries of what is considered normal, acceptable or righteous – are more likely to be scapegoated.

The original scapegoat

The word scapegoat has become common in everyday language; it is used to describe a person who is unfairly blamed for the faults or failures of others. But the term has sacred origins. It first appeared in William Tyndale's 1530 English translation of Leviticus, in which he translated the Hebrew word *azazel* as 'escapegoat'. This gave a vivid image of a sacrificial goat released into the wilderness, bearing the sins of the people. Over time, the letter *e* was dropped and the word 'scapegoat' evolved into the term we use today.

SCAPEGOAT

The concept comes from Leviticus 16, a passage that outlines the ritual for Yom Kippur, the Day of Atonement. This was a day of deep repentance and renewal for the people of Israel. As part of this sacred ritual, the high priest selected two goats: one killed as a sacrifice to God; the other chosen to bear the sins of the people. The high priest laid hands on this second goat's head and confessed over it all the iniquities and transgressions of the community. This act symbolically transferred their sin and shame on to the goat, which was then led out and left in the wilderness alone.

This ritual acts as a sign that the guilt has been removed from the community; and, with this removal of shame, the community is reconciled to God. The first goat's blood atones for the sins of the people, while the scapegoat symbolically carries away the community's shame, enabling cleansing and purification. This image of release is powerful: with their sins removed, the people are cleansed, unburdened of shame and free to begin again. But the cost of this peace is carried by the goat, sent out alone and burdened with the community's collective sin. While the ritual represents forgiveness for the people, the fate of the goat is grim. It is thrown off a cliff or exiled to the wilderness where it is likely to die.

Tyndale's decision to create this new word, 'escapegoat', made this Levitical ritual accessible to English readers and, over time, the term took on a wider meaning. Today, the term 'scapegoat' is used to describe someone who is unjustly blamed, especially in situations where acknowledging the real source of harm would be too painful or disruptive. Scapegoating becomes a way for communities or institutions to preserve a sense of order and dignity. By placing the sins present on to the scapegoat and then sending them away, bearing the shame of the community, they can protect their image and sense of integrity and cohesion. Once the scapegoat is no longer present, it becomes easier to forget or deny what happened. The church community can return to normal, but this is achieved only at the expense of the scapegoat.

From blame to banishment

Survivors who speak up about sexual violence are often seen as a problem because they remind the community of something it doesn't want to face. In refusing to remain silent, they may be perceived as disrupting the stability or moral image of the Church. Their words, even their presence, can come to be seen as a threat. Even when the perpetrator is from outside the group, the community could still feel destabilized.

Survivors can be viewed as a disruptive or uncomfortable presence within the church community. Their ongoing distress can stir feelings of shame or helplessness in others, leading some to wish they would take their pain elsewhere so that a more positive and grateful atmosphere can be restored. Victims may be perceived as tainted or damaged; and, with the discomfort felt, the community may project its guilt and fear on to them.

When recovery does not follow a neat or anticipated timeline, when prayers seem unanswered or legal processes drag on, this discomfort may grow. As a result, survivors can find themselves gradually excluded, no longer invited to events or quietly sidelined in general. Sometimes, they are encouraged to find another community, under the guise that they'd be happier elsewhere; that it would be better for everyone this way.

It can be unspoken. Sometimes, there are just awkward silences, dropped invitations or subtle nudges to move on. Survivors might be excluded from leadership, quietly removed from rotas or told they're too fragile to serve. Sometimes, it's wrapped up in the spiritual language of forgiveness. Survivors may be told that they are being too emotional, too bitter, too angry or too unforgiving. Or, more dangerously, they may be told that they're demonized or carrying a rebellious spirit. Once cast as the problem, it becomes simpler to blame the survivor, easier to discredit them and necessary to exclude them, either actively through church discipline or by ensuring they know they are no longer welcome.

If the perpetrator is one of their own, a leader or a loved and trusted member, then it may feel as if the whole church community is at risk. The person who tells the truth becomes the one blamed for bringing division, for damaging the church and for hurting the ministry. The survivor's disclosure can be seen as a threat not just to a perpetrator's reputation, but also to the church's deeply held beliefs around purity and goodness: 'If this person is guilty, what does that say about us?'

In these moments, scapegoating may emerge as a way to preserve cohesion, with blame shifted on to the victim for the disruption their allegation has caused. Accusations against leaders or well-regarded members are seen not just as personal claims, but also as threats to the community's identity and stability. Power dynamics within churches then work to silence the victim, casting them as damaged, divisive or disloyal; and rumours about their morality or mental health can be used to pour doubt on their words and testimony.

Groups who feel under threat tend to act to protect their reputation and cohesion. Churches, even though they preach a message of truth and justice, are sadly no different. Whether this dynamic happens deliberately or unconsciously, it leads to a lack of empathy for the survivor's suffering and a reshaping of events to deny what happened: to minimize or actively to blame the victim. For those who speak out expecting to be believed and supported, it can be deeply disorienting to find themselves treated as a problem rather than a person in need of care. The difference between church teachings and the treatment victims receive becomes a clashing and confusing dissonance.

A modern-day wilderness

In the previous chapter, we looked at how victim blaming often begins with deeply ingrained cultural scripts, purity culture, honour-based thinking and rape myths. These scripts tell us that if something bad has happened, someone must be at fault. Victim blaming focuses that scrutiny on the individual: what were they wearing? Why didn't they fight back? Why were they alone? But scapegoating goes one step further. It doesn't just assign blame: it assigns responsibility. It places the burden of the group's discomfort, disruption or shame on to the victim; and then, to preserve the illusion of wholeness, the group requires the victim to disappear.

For survivors who have been scapegoated, the wilderness is a lonely place. It can feel like exile from community, from God, even from oneself. They carry not only the weight of what happened to them, but also the shame of how others responded. The very place they expected to find safety becomes a source of harm. Many survivors use the terms 'church hurt' or 're-abuse' to describe this. It's not just the original trauma that wounds them, but the communal response, the silence, the suspicion, the spiritual manipulation. Some describe the reaction to their disclosure as worse than the assault itself. It is hard to overstate how damaging scapegoating can be.

The wilderness might look like social exclusion. It might look like silence, suspicion or spiritualized rejection. A survivor might find themselves blamed for damaging the Church, even though all they did was speak the truth. They may be subtly pressured to move on, leave quietly or withdraw for the good of the Church. Sometimes, they're told to forgive and forget, to let go of bitterness; or that healing can come only through reconciliation with the perpetrator. This places unjust and impossible demands on the victim while letting the community and the perpetrator off the hook. Underneath these responses lies the same old dynamic: 'We can't cope with this. You must carry it away.'

The victim, while feeling that their life has been ripped to pieces and trying to recover from the damage inflicted, now finds that they are being blamed for what happened and pushed out of their community of support and faith. They must carry the weight of the sin inflicted; they must carry the weight of this sin's effect on the church community; they must bear its responsibility; and they must do this alone, out in the wilderness. In removing the survivor, the church can then return to a sense of harmony. But it is a false peace, built on silencing and exile.

Confronting scapegoating

The story of the woman wrongly accused in John 8 offers a profound example of resistance to scapegoating. While often read as a narrative about sin and judging, the passage robustly demonstrates how Jesus confronts group dynamics and stands with the woman against collective condemnation. He refuses to be drawn into their games or to come under their control. He won't join in with the aggressive group behaviour. Instead, he bends down and writes on the ground, an act that disrupts the drama and deflects attention away from the woman. This quiet but powerful gesture invites a pause, a moment of disorientation that breaks the rhythm of escalating violence. When he finally speaks, his words reframe the situation entirely.

> Let anyone among you who is without sin be the first to throw a stone at her. (John 8.7)

With this, Jesus shifts the gaze from the accused to the accusers. Jesus does not argue the woman's innocence. He does not need to as there is no clear evidence against her. He simply refuses to let her be used as an object lesson or a target of public scapegoating. By disrupting the group's behaviour, he dissolves their power; and, one by one, the men leave, their complicity exposed.

What was it that Jesus wrote in the sand that day? It's one of those questions that lingers at the edge of the story, inviting speculation. Preachers have guessed; commentators have theorized: was it a list of sins? Was it the names of the accusers? Or was it something only she could see? Was he simply playing for time, defusing the heat of the crowd before he spoke?

Maybe the not knowing is part of the point. Perhaps the absence of that detail is deliberate, drawing our attention away from the crowd's demands for vengeance and towards something quieter, as the focus shifts from what he wrote to the act of writing itself. A man stooping low, his fingers moving across the dust, while an accused woman stands waiting to die. Everyone else is shouting. Only he and the woman are silent.

THE PIECES JOIN

I find myself returning to that scene again and again, letting it play out in my mind. I see her, a woman dragged from somewhere: perhaps from her home, perhaps from the streets. She has no name, no voice, no words to defend herself; there is only the noise of those who accuse her. She's been taken, brought out into the open, exposed; her fate now a public spectacle. The crowd are gathered, angry, self-righteous; stones ready in their hands, when another figure steps into view. He looks like them: he's a man, a rabbi, but something in his posture sets him apart. He isn't shouting. He isn't jeering. He doesn't throw her to the ground or demand her confession. Instead, he lowers himself to the dust beside her, kneels in the same dirt they've kicked up, and starts to write. And I wonder, did he write it for her? Maybe it was a message no one else could read: a message scratched in the dust and gone with the next gust of wind. Maybe he wrote, 'You're not alone.' Maybe he wrote, 'Trust me.' Maybe he wrote, 'I'm going to save you.'

I find myself wondering what Jesus saw when he looked into her eyes. I wonder if, as he stood between her and the men who wanted her dead, Jesus thought of his own mother and saw the fragile thread that held his own story together. Mary had been young, unmarried and pregnant. Her life had been in danger too, and with it, his. Maybe he saw in this woman an image of the woman who had once carried him, the woman who had once faced death because of the appearance of sin. Maybe he knew what to do in this moment because he had heard how his father Joseph had acted to save them.

Jesus' actions challenge the dynamic of the moment and the crowd. He centres the victim, refusing to join the spectacle. He challenges the self-righteousness of the group, exposing how easily violence can be cloaked in moral language. And finally, he speaks to the woman directly, not as an object of sin, of pity or scrutiny, but as a person:

'Woman, where are they? Has no one condemned you?' ...
'No one, sir.'...
'Neither do I condemn you.' (John 8.10–11)

SCAPEGOAT

These words of restoration neither shame her nor deny her agency; and he sends her on her way, free to take up her life again. This passage not only gives an alternative to scapegoating behaviour, but also calls us to resist easy narratives, to dismantle group mentalities, and to make space to hear and believe the voices and accounts of victims. It is an invitation to act like Jesus, to disrupt the spectacle, to refuse the stone and to stand with the one left in the dust.

5

Justice

The phone rings. I check. It looks as if it's the police. I get up from the floor, stepping on Lego as I make my way to the quiet of the kitchen. The ringing of the phone jars; it crashes my senses. My brain is doing the thing where everything moves slowly and quickly at the same time. I tell myself it's OK: it's just the adrenaline. I tell myself that this is just the monthly police update. This won't be new information. It's just them kindly telling me that there is nothing to update yet: they're still waiting for digital evidence. I ask them to hold on for a moment; I give myself time to slump into the corner chair, readying myself.

The tone is different this time: his voice is upbeat. I'm not catching everything he's saying, but finally things have progressed. I have to ask him to slow down and go through it again. The words are jumping around like bubbles; I'm trying to catch them, but they disappear if I move too fast. I open my hand, and a large bubble comes to rest; it sits still and round and glistening on my outstretched hand.

It's going to trial.

He's talking again: outlining the reasons why; what evidence they have found; the confession they have obtained; and that they are confident going forward. The words are getting jumbled up again, disappearing as quickly as they appear. I concentrate on the imaginary bubble on my hand: it's still and fragile and, for a moment, beautiful.

We're going to trial.

I don't respond, sitting here, looking around the kitchen. Everything is the same: the cat curled up in the corner; the mugs out waiting for tea. Nothing is different from ten minutes ago,

JUSTICE

but everything has changed. I don't dare move: I don't want this bubble to pop. Somewhere in the distance he is asking me something, repeating it, needing a response. He's optimistic, cheerful even. He's expecting more from me in this moment; more than silence. An infographic I saw somewhere, displaying reporting and conviction rates, lights up in my brain. Of all those little people lined up, I'm the lucky one in the bottom right-hand corner. I tell myself I'm one of the lucky ones. I know I'm one of the lucky ones. I tell myself I'm one of the lucky ones. I don't feel lucky.

For every 100 rape victims, it is estimated

84 do not report to the police

16 do report to the police

From this
0.5 will make it to trial
0.3 will result in a conviction

Figure 1: Estimated reporting and conviction rates[1]

---

[1] Infographic based on estimated reporting and conviction rates for rape in England and Wales from the Crown Prosecution Service and crime outcome reporting. Rates for sexual assault are trickier to estimate.

THE PIECES JOIN

Justice delayed and justice denied

This chapter traces the long, narrowing path from a sexual assault to a courtroom verdict and shows just how sharply the system thins out the chances of justice. It's estimated that only 16 in every 100 victims of rape ever speak to the police; only a handful of those cases are passed to prosecutors; fewer than 1 in every 100 reaches trial or secures a conviction. This leaves us with many questions.

Why do so many survivors feel unable, or unsafe, to report at all? For those who find the courage to do so, why does the investigatory process stretch on for months or years, draining hope and forcing painful choices that increase dropout rates and fracture families? Why are prosecutors so reluctant to take cases forward and juries hesitant to convict, despite the prevalence of assault? Where does this leave victims and survivors when the justice almost never arrives?

Low reporting rates

Many survivors do not report to the police. The reasons are multiple and complex, personal and societal; but victim accounts show themes and patterns in the causes and reasons why they do not report. The following examples are based on anonymized victim accounts; they explore some of the reasons why so few victims report the crimes committed against them.

The fear of not being believed

Emma had been assaulted by a colleague who was widely respected. She'd watched what happened when another woman spoke up: how quickly she was dismissed, whispered about and quietly frozen out. 'No one will believe me,' Emma thought. She stayed silent.

JUSTICE

Victim blaming

Sarah told a friend what had happened to her at a party. Her friend's first question was 'How much had you had to drink?' That single sentence was enough to plant doubt – not just about the night in question, but about whether Sarah herself was somehow to blame. She didn't tell anyone else.

Psychological impact

Mark struggled even to describe the assault. Whenever he tried, his throat would close, panic would rise and he'd start to shake. The thought of speaking to numerous officers, retelling the story again and again, felt impossible. He kept the trauma inside and, with it, the shame.

Problems at the police station

Leah went to the police station, with the intention of reporting. She'd rehearsed what she would say and brought a friend for support. But when she arrived, she was asked to wait in the main reception area, where she sat for over an hour. When someone finally came to speak to her, it was a uniformed male officer; he told her she'd need to come back another day to speak with someone from the right department. No one took her details. 'I felt like an inconvenience,' she said. 'I left thinking, maybe it wasn't serious enough to bother them. I just didn't go back.'

Fear of retaliation

Alex feared what would happen if they did speak out. Their perpetrator was part of a close-knit friendship group, all active on social media. Alex had seen what happened to others who called out abuse: trolling, threats, public humiliation. They didn't want to be the next one torn apart.

Social stigma

Lisa was afraid of what her church would say. She had been in a relationship with her boyfriend for some time before he raped her. In her church community, remaining pure was highly valued and reputations meant everything. She feared being seen as damaged or, worse, being blamed for letting things go too far. She prayed; she cried. But she didn't go to the police.

Power dynamics and authority

Hannah's abuser was a trusted elder in her congregation. She feared that speaking out would mean being disbelieved, isolated or even spiritually condemned. The power imbalance felt too great to challenge. She chose to leave the church rather than report the man who had harmed her.

Fear of damaging the faith community

Keisha was assaulted by a fellow churchgoer; but she hesitated to report it because she worried it would create division within her tight-knit faith community. She feared being blamed for bringing scandal to the church and potentially driving members away.

Pressure and reputation management

David reported being assaulted to the church leadership, expecting support and action. Instead, he was told to keep quiet and pray for healing, as the church wanted to prevent negative publicity.

Community loyalty

Jade was assaulted by a prominent church member. She wanted to report but had a strong sense of commitment and loyalty to the church. She didn't want to tarnish its image, so she decided to stay quiet.

JUSTICE

Secrecy and internal handling

Sam's church had a policy of handling such matters internally. When they disclosed the abuse, the church conducted its own investigation and decided not to involve law enforcement.

Religious belief

Jess was taught to forgive and turn the other cheek as part of her religious upbringing. When she was assaulted, these teachings made her feel conflicted about seeking justice: she believed it was more righteous to forgive her abuser.

Spiritual and emotional manipulation

Jacob, a student and new at church, was assaulted by a priest who used religious language to justify the abuse. The abuser claimed it was part of a divine plan, leaving Jacob confused and ashamed.

Lack of trust in the police

Nina had been assaulted by someone she knew from her local community. She never reported the attack. Years earlier, when her cousin had gone to the police after experiencing domestic abuse, the officers had been dismissive and suggested that she might have provoked it. Nina hadn't forgotten. She didn't trust the police to take her seriously or to protect her if she came forward. 'I knew how they looked at us,' she said. 'If I walked into that station, I'd be the one under suspicion.'

These different elements created significant barriers for victims, making it difficult for them to report abuse and achieve justice.

Reporting, evidence collection and delays

Those who do report face a system that is often painfully slow and retraumatizing; and each stage of that system contains critical pressure points where cases quietly fall away. Phones and laptops are seized for months, while digital backlogs build. Overstretched officers and prosecutors must meet a high evidential threshold, so files are returned for more evidence or marked as having no realistic prospect of conviction. With the few cases that do reach the threshold to go to trial, court listings stretch into years; during that time, some victims decide to move on with their lives and do not want to revisit the trauma by going to trial. Therapy notes and private messages may be requested under disclosure rules, which can feel like another violation and causes victims to question whether they want to proceed.

Phone seizure and delays

Susie reported her rape and handed over her phone, as requested. She didn't get it back for more than 14 months. During that time, she lost her job and began to feel as if she'd lost her life too: everything was on hold. Eventually, she stopped responding to police updates. The case was closed due to victim non-engagement.

Victim privacy and access to therapy notes

Bea reported the assault but was later told that the defence would need access to private therapy notes. Those notes held the most vulnerable parts of her: thoughts she hadn't shared with anyone else. When she refused to give consent, the Crown Prosecution Service (CPS) dropped the case. It was deemed not winnable.

Evidential difficulties

Maria reported her rape within hours. She had bruises and reported where it took place. But the CCTV was of poor quality and the toxicology inconclusive. Without more forensic evidence, the police said there wasn't enough to proceed. Maria was told she'd been brave; but being told she was brave didn't equal receiving justice.

Backlog and court delays

Ella waited more than three years for her case to come to court. By the time a trial date arrived, she had moved cities, started a new relationship and was about to have a baby. The thought of going through a public trial while heavily pregnant was too much. She withdrew, apologetically. Her case was one of hundreds that year that collapsed under the weight of delay.

Spiritual abuse and coercion

Ruth was in her 20s when her pastor began grooming her. He told her that God had chosen her for something special: a spiritual connection that included sexual intimacy. She was confused and ashamed; she eventually went to the police. But the case was logged as consensual sex between adults and the coercion was difficult to prove in legal terms. The case was dropped. She was left feeling spiritually violated and legally invisible.

Delays and evidence gathering

Samir's case involved a known perpetrator: someone already on the radar. The police submitted a file to the CPS. After delays, the CPS asked for more evidence. The submission of extra evidence was, in turn, delayed due to staff shortages. After nine more months, during which time Samir's mental health worsened, a new CPS lawyer reviewed the file and concluded it didn't meet the public interest threshold. It never went to court.

Legal and evidentiary challenges

Maggie reported her assault immediately. But there was little physical evidence and her attacker claimed the encounter was consensual. The case relied heavily on 'he said, she said' testimonies, making it hard to achieve a conviction, so it was dropped by the CPS.

Lack of trust in the legal system

Sasha reported her assault to the police, but the investigation was slow: she was not updated about progress and thought it was not properly investigated. After two years, she heard that the case wasn't going to trial owing to insufficient evidence. This left Sasha feeling that the legal system was not on her side.

Going to trial

For the small number of victims who do make it to trial, the experience is rarely one of relief or resolution. On average, at least two years would have passed since they reported the crime. Sometimes, it takes much longer. As I sit here writing in 2025, the trial of Chris Brain, the former leader of the Nine O'Clock Service, is happening at the Inner London Crown Court. It has taken more than 30 years for this case to come to trial.

When survivors reach court, they often face an adversarial courtroom culture shaped by myths and stereotypes about rape. Juries may expect to see physical injury, emotional collapse or clear evidence of resistance. These assumptions bear little resemblance to how trauma actually works.

Survivors are routinely questioned about their clothing, drinking, relationships and sexual history. Rather than the accused being on trial, it is often the victim's character and credibility that are scrutinized.

JUSTICE

Jo had reported a violent sexual assault by the man who led her Bible study group at church. At trial, the defence focused on the fact that she had gone back to his flat, suggesting this showed mixed signals. They asked detailed questions about her underwear, how many sexual partners she had previously had, and whether she had regretted the encounter. Despite forensic evidence of injury, the jury returned a not guilty verdict. Jo said the trial felt more violating than the assault itself.

Rachel was a student when she reported being raped by someone in her wider social circle. The case took two years to come to court. On the stand, she was cross-examined for nearly four hours, asked repeatedly why she hadn't screamed, why she hadn't fought back and why she had sent the perpetrator a message a week later about a group project. 'I wanted to be believed,' she said afterwards. 'But it felt like I had to perform trauma in a way that fitted their script.' The jury couldn't reach a verdict and the CPS chose not to pursue a retrial.

Nazir gave evidence in a trial involving historic abuse by a family member. Although corroborating evidence had been gathered from others, he was questioned aggressively about why he hadn't spoken up earlier and whether he might have misremembered events. The defence implied that he was bitter and seeking revenge. After a conviction was secured, Nazir described the win as 'hollow'. 'It proved I wasn't lying,' he said. 'But I don't know if I'd survive it again.'

These stories show that even when a case reaches trial, the courtroom is not a place of safety or truth. The process is adversarial by design and often focused on discrediting the survivor. Myths about real victims, assumptions about memory, and prejudices around gender, race, class or sexuality continue to shape how evidence is received. For many survivors, the experience of giving evidence is itself a form of trauma. Even when convictions are secured, survivors can be left feeling exposed, diminished, or broken by what they endured in court. Justice, if it comes, is often partial and painfully won.

A rare outcome

I know from personal experience that the criminal justice system can work. I am one of the few for whom it did. To be honest, I feel a little nervous writing about it. I don't want to give the impression that it worked out because I approached it correctly. That isn't how it works. But I do think it's important to share the stories of when justice is achieved, because there are things we can learn from that too.

Reporting was never going to be easy, but I was met with compassion, clarity and professionalism at every stage. The police were supportive and thorough in taking my statement and collecting evidence. They stayed in contact and offered regular updates. There were delays, but the regular updates meant I knew the case had not just been forgotten. Their work led not only to my case going to trial but also, as is so rarely the case, to a conviction.

I was also lucky. Incredibly lucky. Things lined up in ways that I know they often don't. As the investigation unfolded, the police uncovered evidence of more than 25 other assaults carried out by the same perpetrator. From those, they were able to link him to three other reported crimes, one of which was included in the trial alongside my case. He was convicted and received the longest sentence ever given for that type of crime. After the conviction, he went to the Court of Appeal about the length of the sentence. It felt as if I were being dragged back through a system I thought had been finalized. But, in the end, the conviction was upheld.

I know that when the system works, it can bring some measure of justice; not only for the individual survivor but for others too. But I also know that my experience is the exception. The fact that it worked for me still only highlights how rarely that happens. In my own case, there was clear evidence that others had been harmed too: other women who never got their day in court and who never heard that he was eventually convicted.

It shouldn't take luck. Justice shouldn't be conditional on everything coming together exactly. It shouldn't be unusual for a survivor to be believed, supported and see their case taken seriously. The problem is not that the system never works, but that it doesn't work often enough: far too many victims are left with nothing.

A few months after the trial, I was catching up with a colleague who had known about the assault. They are nice and well meaning; if you asked them, they would probably even say they have been a support to me. But when I told them about the conviction, their initial response was to say, 'So, it really did happen then.'

That was years ago now; but it's hard to forget a response like that. Given that we have a justice system that convicts in so, so few cases, we must find other ways of speaking to and supporting victims. Statistically speaking, crimes of sexual assault are unlikely to make it to court. With fewer than one per cent of rapes resulting in a conviction, this cannot be the qualifier for us to believe whether something *really did happen*.

If justice fails, what then?

For many survivors, engaging with the criminal justice system becomes an extension of the trauma rather than a path to recovery: more rips and tears to add to the challenges that they have already encountered. The process is often long, opaque and emotionally exhausting. Even those who begin with hope and resolve can find themselves slowly worn down by delays, requests for intrusive evidence or a lack of communication. Some describe living in limbo for months or years, unable to move forward, with no sense of resolution in sight. Their lives are put on hold while they wait for updates, for decisions, for trial dates that may never come.

Being asked to hand over private phones, therapy records or social media conversations can feel like another violation.

Survivors may comply in good faith, trusting that these requests are necessary, only to discover later that the material was used to undermine their credibility or that their case was dropped regardless. In the worst moments, the process itself begins to mirror the abuse: an experience of being disempowered, disbelieved and exposed without protection.

Victims of sexual assault are pushed to meet impossible standards just to be heard. They should be calm but not cold, emotional but not hysterical, sexually inexperienced but not ashamed. The adversarial courtroom intensifies this pressure. Cross-examination can flip from seeking truth to putting the victim's life choices, clothing, alcohol intake and post-assault reactions on trial. To be believed they must appear perfect, almost above questioning, untouched by the ordinary inconsistencies of being human. But a system that demands such perfection from victims is no system of justice at all. True justice must make space for real people, not idealized victims.

When cases are delayed or fall apart, the impact ripples far beyond the individual. Survivors are often left to explain to their families, workplaces or church communities what happened and why justice was not possible. In faith settings especially, where issues of shame, silence and power are already complex, the decision to report can fracture relationships and leave survivors further isolated. Some leave their communities altogether. Others stay but remain silent, watching how the institution treats those who speak.

In the absence of a just outcome, survivors are left to make sense of their own experience, without public acknowledgement of wrongdoing. Some seek alternative forms of justice: restorative meetings, civil action, safeguarding investigations; or they simply tell their story in spaces where it can be heard and held. These routes are not perfect, but they offer something the criminal justice system often cannot: a sense of agency, validation and the possibility of being heard.

And yet, amid all of this, many survivors still find the courage to speak. Their testimonies – shared in courtrooms, churches, media interviews or private conversations – have driven reform.

JUSTICE

Survivor-led advocacy has shaped public awareness, challenged harmful myths, and brought about tangible change in police practices and court procedures. The justice system may remain broken in many places, but survivors are not waiting passively for it to fix itself. They are still speaking; still standing; still imagining something better.

6

Perfect Victims

It's 7.30 on Sunday morning; I'm standing in front of the vestry desk preparing for the first service of the day. My eyes skim over the service sheet.

'A full, perfect, and sufficient sacrifice, oblation and satisfaction.'

I remind myself to breathe.

'A full, perfect, and sufficient sacrifice, oblation and satisfaction.'

I whisper the words under my breath. Rolling them over my tongue until the shape of them lodges in my memory.

'A full, perfect, and sufficient sacrifice, oblation and satisfaction.'

Soon I'll be saying this from behind the altar; and I need to be able to get the words out without tripping over them. The 1662 Book of Common Prayer liturgy and its old-style words sometimes trip you up, especially if you're masking a lisp or you have trouble saying 'th'. But that wasn't what was happening here. Last time I led this service, I got stuck on the word 'perfect'. It's not even difficult to say. I try again.

'A full, *perfect*, and sufficient sacrifice, oblation and satisfaction.'

The last time I stood behind the altar, falling over my words, the detective sergeant's voice echoed around the chapel: 'You're the perfect victim. Can't you see? You are the perfect victim.'

He was right. He was only stating the obvious. The way the assault had occurred, the way the evidence had fallen into place, who I was and how it could be presented in court all meant that no barrister, however accomplished, could raise doubt about my character or actions. While the evidence they had collected pointed to more than 25 victims, it would hang on my evidence. Given the circumstances, I was about as perfect a victim as could be.

Perfect

'Perfect' is one of those words that carries a lot of weight. It can sound reassuring, even comforting. But 'perfect' can also be a heavy and demanding word. And depending on where and how it's used, it can mean very different things.

'Perfect' is sometimes taken to mean 'pure': the religious version that often gets tangled up with purity culture or harsh moral expectations. That kind of perfect means – if you've made any wrong decisions, if your story is complicated, if you've had sex, doubted, struggled or broken down – you're no longer pure. It can leave people feeling as if they must scrub their stories clean before coming anywhere near God.

In the courtroom, victims are held up to the standard of a perfect victim: a victim who not only did the right things but was the right kind of person – pure and innocent. It's not just about being truthful: it's about appearing untouched, innocent in every possible sense; morally clean, emotionally controlled. Sometimes perfect means flawless, spotless, without a single mistake. Survivors of sexual assault are expected to be calm but not cold, emotional but not angry, entirely composed and totally credible. Basically, superhuman. If they slip up or show any messiness, they risk being disbelieved.

Church teaching describes Jesus as the perfect sacrifice: a sinless and innocent man; the perfect victim. And it goes further, even saying that justice required a perfect victim to act as the perfect sacrifice. Theologically, 'perfect' can also mean complete or whole when used to describe God's work at the Cross. But it can be tricky to distinguish between these meanings when the word takes on different forms.

How we speak about the Cross and how we describe salvation

matters, especially for those who have experienced violence firsthand. For survivors of abuse, the Church's language of salvation can sometimes echo the very harm they have endured. Those who have experienced violence and violation can find both comfort and horror in the concept and imagery of a faith that holds the violation of God at its centre. The language of salvation is never neutral: it is shaped by theology, culture and power. For survivors, it intersects deeply with the realities of trauma, injustice and survival. When someone has experienced violence, been blamed for it and then dismissed by the justice system, the Church's way of talking about salvation can easily alienate rather than affirm. Even the mechanics of how we talk about salvation – the use of terms such as 'innocence' and 'shame', 'violence' and 'victimhood', 'sin' and 'separation from God' – can mirror the dynamics of abuse. And yet, if we are willing to listen carefully and speak honestly, there may still be something within these concepts and beliefs that points towards the possibility of recovery and repair.

How Christians have understood the Cross

At the heart of Christian faith stands a crucified Christ. The question of how Christ's death brings reconciliation between God and humanity has shaped Christian theology from its earliest days. Over time, different theories of atonement have emerged, each offering a distinct lens through which to understand the mystery of the Cross.

These theories are not mutually exclusive. Most worshippers today draw intuitively on a blend of them. Yet each theory reflects particular theological concerns and cultural contexts; and each shapes how we speak of God, justice, suffering and salvation. In recent decades, theologians – particularly feminist, liberationist and trauma-informed voices – have re-examined traditional atonement models, challenged harmful implications and sought new ways to understand the Cross in the light of human dignity and experience. But before looking at these, perhaps it is helpful to remember that there is not one way of talking about the Cross or of describing salvation. So, let's look at the range of perspectives that have developed across the Church.

The earliest Christian understanding of the Cross focused less on sin and guilt, and more on deliverance. Jesus' death and Resurrection were seen as a dramatic battle in which Christ the Victor defeated the powers of evil. Rooted in New Testament texts, such as Colossians 2.15 and 1 Corinthians 15.54–57, this view dominated the early Church. It portrays Christ as the conquering hero who overcomes every force that enslaves humanity. Jesus, by becoming human, enters the realm of death and bursts it open from within. More recently, the image of the victorious Christ has been explored by theologians concerned with oppression and liberation. For survivors of trauma and abuse, it offers a vision of a God who stands against destructive power and fights for deliverance.

Another concept that dominated early Christian thought is referred to as ransom theory. It draws on Jesus' words in Mark's Gospel: 'For the Son of Man came ... to give his life a ransom for many' (Mark 10.45). This is the idea that Christ's death was a kind of transaction, a ransom paid, though the question of to whom the ransom was paid has varied. Early theologians, such as Origen and Gregory of Nyssa, speculated that the ransom was paid to Satan, who held humanity captive through sin and death. Later generations found this problematic – why would God negotiate with the devil? Still, the core idea of liberation through cost remained influential. While modern theologians tend to reject the literal idea of God bargaining with Satan, the metaphor of freedom through costly love remains powerful. The model affirms that something real is at stake in human suffering and that God goes to profound lengths to set us free.

In the eleventh century, Anselm of Canterbury reimagined the atonement through feudal imagery in his satisfaction theory. Sin, he argued, dishonours God's majesty and creates a debt of honour that humanity cannot repay. Christ, both divine and human, offers satisfaction on our behalf, restoring the moral order. This model laid the groundwork for later legal interpretations, most notably the penal substitution theory developed during the Reformation by Calvin. Shifting from feudal to courtroom imagery, Calvin framed sin as a breach of law demanding punishment – death. Christ becomes our substitute, taking the penalty in our place to satisfy God's justice. While both models emphasize justice and divine mercy, they raise troubling questions: do they portray God as requiring violence to forgive? Can suffering be redemptive? Does justice achieved through substitution risk sanctifying abuse? These concerns have led many theologians and survivors alike to seek models of atonement that uphold both justice and mercy without relying on punitive or violent frameworks.

Abelard, in the twelfth century, proposed that Christ's death is not a transaction by which God's wrath was assuaged, but a demonstration of divine love so powerful it moves the human heart to repentance and transformation. This moral influence theory emphasizes the ethical and relational impact of the Cross. In seeing Christ's love, we are drawn into love ourselves. Atonement, therefore, is not about satisfying divine demands: it's about healing alienation and renewing relationship. This resonates with those who have experienced the Cross as a place of solidarity and compassion. It avoids violent or punitive language and places responsibility for change with us. Critics argue that it may underestimate the seriousness of sin or the need for justice, but it remains an important corrective to transactional views.

More recently, particularly through the work of René Girard (2001), the scapegoat theory of atonement has emerged as a powerful way of understanding the Cross. Drawing on the imagery of the scapegoat in Leviticus, Girard observes that cultures often preserve peace by blaming and expelling a scapegoat: someone marked as *other*, on to whom the community projects its fear, guilt or rage. Jesus, the innocent one, is crucified by the crowd. But he does not respond with revenge and thereby unmasks the whole violent system. The Cross becomes not a demand for blood but a revelation of how much damage we do when we justify harm in the name of order or holiness. For survivors of abuse or exclusion, this model offers deep resonance: it tells the truth about victimization, something they have experienced first-hand. It rejects the myth that suffering is redemptive; and it locates God not with the accusers, but with the one cast out. Contemporary theologians have developed models rooted in solidarity, emphasizing that, in the Cross, Christ suffers with us (Moltmann, 1974). For trauma theologians, such as Shelly Rambo (2010), the power of the Cross lies not in resolving suffering but in staying present to it. Christ enters the depths of death, trauma and abandonment, and still breathes peace. James Cone (2011) interprets the Cross in light of the lynching tree, emphasizing that Jesus was crucified among the oppressed; and his death exposes the injustice of systems that crucify again and again. For survivors of abuse, for those harmed by church power or for those silenced by systems of control, the idea of God's solidarity is transformative. It tells us that God is not the punisher but the one crucified; God is not the accuser but the scapegoat.

More than one way to the Cross

Theories of atonement are not abstract ideas. They shape how we imagine God and how we speak about sin, salvation and ourselves. They have the power to liberate or to harm, depending on how they are preached and lived. While no single theory captures the full mystery of the Cross, taken together they remind us that atonement is not about satisfying divine wrath but revealing divine love: a love strong enough to confront sin, enter suffering, unmask scapegoating and offer resurrection. In a world marked by injustice, trauma and the misuse of power, the work of atonement remains unfinished – not because Christ's work is lacking, but because we are still learning to live into its meaning.

Each classical or contemporary atonement model throws light on the Cross from a different angle; and survivors of sexual assault often find themselves drawn to some rays while shielding their eyes from others. Christ victorious celebrates liberation from powers that enslave. Victims may hear this as a God who storms the stronghold of abuse and sets captives free. Yet the martial language can mask the intimate wounds of a single violated body. Ransom keeps the note of costly rescue but risks picturing victims as chips in a celestial bargain. For someone who has already been treated like an object, that metaphor may sting more than soothe.

Satisfaction theory and its Reformation cousin penal substitution speak of justice taken seriously. Survivors may welcome that moral clarity. But the danger comes when these models slip into idealizing sacrificial violence, as if bloodshed itself pleases God. A victim who has already been told that her suffering will bring good in the end can find such preaching retraumatizing, even if the preacher's intent is quite the opposite.

Moral-influence theories move the focus to love's persuasive power. The Cross softens hardened hearts and calls communities to repentance. This gentler and transformative take on the Cross avoids glorifying pain but risks underestimating the depth of harm. Victims may find the focus on transformation at best naïve while perpetrators remain unrepentant and unaccountable. By contrast, a focus on God's solidarity with us insists that God stands inside the experience of trauma, refusing to abandon the violated. While not romanticizing abuse, this focus locates God's presence precisely where churches have often been absent.

The scapegoat theory names what many survivors recognize instinctively: communities preserve their innocence by casting blame on to a vulnerable body. The Cross unmasks that lie and announces divine solidarity with the one shoved outside the camp. Yet even here care is needed. Christ's power to upend systemic violence, within himself and without revenge, can be communicated and heard as the call to embrace victimhood rather than reclaim agency.

The Scriptures offer more than one perspective on salvation. While this may lack the clarity or simplicity some might prefer, it honours both the richness of the Church's teaching and the lived experience of victims and survivors. Holding space for these varied perspectives allows different truths to be heard; and, through them, the good news of liberation can begin to take shape. Atonement theology becomes life-giving when churches hold on to these multiple lenses: it allows victims to approach the Cross without having to fit a single script; and it refuses any telling of salvation that turns violence itself into something holy. True good news invites victims towards recovery, challenges the Church to pull apart beliefs that glorify violence, and engages in the hard work of dismantling patterns and systems of harm that continue to crucify.

No one takes it from me

Jesus said:

> I am the good shepherd. The good shepherd lays down his life for the sheep. The hired hand, who is not the shepherd and does not own the sheep, sees the wolf coming and leaves the sheep and runs away – and the wolf snatches them and scatters them ... I lay down my life in order to take it up again. No one takes it from me, but I lay it down of my own accord. I have power to lay it down, and I have power to take it up again. (John 10.11, 12, 17 and 18)

Whenever we talk about salvation, we are also talking about power. The dynamics of who acts, who decides, who is harmed and who is believed are not just abstract questions: they are also deeply personal questions, especially so for victims and survivors of violence. When the Church speaks of the Cross, and when it uses the language of sacrifice and suffering, it must tread carefully. Too often, portrayals of salvation have romanticized victimhood, glorified pain or suggested that suffering itself is holy. For survivors who have already had their agency taken from them, these messages are not just unhelpful: they can also be profoundly damaging.

When the writers of John's Gospel compiled and edited the stories of Jesus to make sense of his life, death and Resurrection, it was important to them to show Jesus' agency; John 10.18 is an example of this. Jesus does not go passively to the Cross. He is not overpowered, manipulated or sacrificed by others without consent. He lays down his life willingly and will take it back up. This image is offered in contrast to the sheep who, at the will and violence of the wolf, are unable to protect themselves or determine their fate. This act of self-giving love is central to the gospel; but it is Jesus' to give. No one takes it from him. That distinction mattered to those early disciples and still matters today.

Jesus, a victim of sexual abuse?

In 2021, Reaves, Tombs and Figueroa brought together a range of theologians, academics and practitioners to write about Jesus as a victim of sexual abuse. The resulting book, *When Did We See You Naked? Jesus as a Victim of Sexual Abuse* is a collection of biblical reflections, theology, poetry and personal accounts that asks a deeply uncomfortable but important question: was Jesus sexually abused? The intention wasn't to shock, but to invite a more honest look at the reality of crucifixion. Jesus was stripped, exposed, mocked and publicly shamed: acts that, in any other context, we would recognize as sexualized violence.

The book draws on a wide range of voices from different parts of the world: some writing as scholars, others as survivors; some as both. Some contributors reflect on how this view changes our understanding of atonement and suffering; others ask what it might mean for survivors to see their own experience reflected in Christ's story.

The response to *When Did We See You Naked?* has been intense; at times, almost visceral. I remember being in an online seminar with one of the authors, recounting the reactions on Twitter. Among survivors of sexual violence, reactions were sharply divided. Some found deep comfort in seeing Jesus named as a victim of sexual abuse: a Christ who knows, from the inside, the shame, the stripping, the forced exposure and violation; a Jesus who has been where they have been. For them, this naming brought unexpected solidarity and spiritual recognition: he was not just a Saviour who suffered for them, but one who had suffered with them.

But others found the idea profoundly disturbing, even offensive. For some, naming Jesus as a victim of abuse undermined their image of him as strong, dignified and in control. While they could accept that he had been stripped, mocked, tortured and murdered, to frame these acts as sexual abuse introduced a power dynamic they could not reconcile with their theology. Their Jesus had agency. He laid down his life of his own accord. He chose the path to the Cross. To describe him as a victim of abuse risked, for them, diminishing that divine authority.

This tension points to a deeper theological question: can power and victimhood coexist? For some, the very notion of abuse implies helplessness, violation without consent: an unbearable idea when applied to Jesus. But for others, it is precisely in the vulnerability of Jesus – publicly stripped, taunted, exposed, unable to move or cover himself – that they find the courage to name their own stories. The discomfort many felt was not just theological but emotional, even bodily. The Cross has always been unsettling. But when seen through the lens of sexual violence, it challenges not only our theology of suffering but our assumptions about power, dignity and the meaning of salvation itself.

These differing responses also expose the tensions running through atonement theology. Some atonement language emphasizes agency: Christ choosing to suffer, offering himself as a sacrifice, laying down his life freely. This sits comfortably with models, such as satisfaction theory or penal substitution, that depend on Jesus as an active participant who chooses to bear the weight of sin. But for those who experience the Cross as a place of violation – where Jesus is stripped, mocked, exposed and rendered powerless – these models can feel jarring or even complicit in glorifying violence. The suggestion that suffering is salvific, or that God requires it, risks aligning divine action with the logic of abuse.

Scapegoat theory and atonement as solidarity create space to hold both vulnerability and agency together. They invite us to see Jesus not as a passive victim, but as one who exposes the mechanisms of blame, shame and power that underpin both crucifixion and abuse. The Cross is not the place of divine punishment for human violence but God's refusal to collude with it. Salvation begins not with idealized sacrifice, but with truth-telling, solidarity and resistance. For survivors, this can be life-giving theology. It says: 'Your suffering was not redemptive, but it is seen.' God does not require it, but God knows it.

The Church must tread with care when it speaks of the Cross. Survivors are listening. What kind of God are we proclaiming? If our liturgies imply that suffering is required, that pain is pleasing to God or that victims must endure in silence for a greater good, we risk retraumatizing those who have already borne too much. This requires careful language and trauma-aware preaching. It also means that we must stop asking survivors to find redemption in what harmed them. Instead, we are called to be communities where their stories are honoured, their anger is not pathologized and their presence is not conditional on forgiveness or silence.

7

Finding Absolution

We've looked at the complex challenges survivors often face: the initial trauma of abuse; the subsequent victim blaming; the isolating cruelty of scapegoating; and the enduring impact of a dysfunctional system of criminal justice. Some survivors of abuse take the understandable decision to stay away from church, keeping their distance to protect themselves. Perhaps more surprisingly, some victims report the importance of their faith in navigating a way through their experiences. They want to remain part of the Church, perhaps by trying other churches, searching for somewhere that feels safe enough. But for these survivors who want to continue to practise their faith, attending church, reading the Bible and engaging in worship may be agonizingly complicated. How can the resources and practices of faith, which were present within the abuse, be part of the path to recovery?

In the previous chapter, we began to explore how we understand and communicate the violence of the Cross. In this chapter, I will explore how the common church practices of confession and absolution may be experienced by survivors; and, in doing so, I will suggest some ways in which churches can support victims.[1] By recognizing the effects of our words and practices, and by conducting worship with this awareness, churches may be able to reduce the retraumatizing that survivors can experience in worship settings.

---

1 I first presented this material at the 'Abusing God: Reading the Bible in the #MeToo Age' Colloquium as part of the Abuse in Religious Contexts Project (funded by the Arts and Humanities Research Council), at Manchester University in September 2022.

Confession and absolution within public worship

You may have heard the gospel described like this: we have sinned; this divides us from God; we feel sinful and ashamed. Jesus died for us; and if we confess our sins, God forgives us and we are reconciled with God again. While different churches may express this teaching in distinctive ways, this is broadly the teaching of the Church across the breadth of traditions. It is embedded in the practice of confession within Christian worship, with churches often having set times of communal confession and absolution within services. This could be formally or liturgically organized, with set words and prayers, or more free-flowing, depending on church tradition. But either way, the congregation will be encouraged to bring their sin before God and receive assurance that their sins are forgiven. Below is an example of a congregational prayer of confession, followed by a prayer of absolution, regularly used in the Church of England. Here, sin is taken to mean wrongful actions committed, both deliberately and through weakness, and omissions to act.

Confession

Almighty God, our heavenly Father,
we have sinned against you
and against our neighbour
in thought and word and deed,
through negligence, through weakness,
through our own deliberate fault.
We are truly sorry
and repent of all our sins.
For the sake of your Son Jesus Christ,
who died for us,
forgive us all that is past
and grant that we may serve you in newness of life
to the glory of your name.
Amen.

Absolution

Almighty God,
who forgives all who truly repent,
have mercy upon you,
pardon and deliver you from all your sins,
confirm and strengthen you in all goodness,
and keep you in life eternal;
through Jesus Christ our Lord.
Amen.
(*Common Worship*, 2000, pp. 169–70)

The term 'sin' is rarely heard outside church settings; but it is often used in public worship, in times of confession and absolution, in readings and teaching, and in hymns and worship songs. 'Sin' is often bound together with the word 'shame'. But what do we understand of these terms and what is happening when we engage in acts of communal confession and absolution?

Simplistically, we might say that sin refers to the things we do that are wrong: deliberately, through weakness or by failing to act. Guilt is our conscience telling us we have done something wrong; and shame is the uncomfortable feeling we associate with the wrongdoing. In worship, we may be encouraged to recall our acts of wrongdoing, to feel the guilt and shame in recalling our sins, and to experience a sense of peace or reconnection with God as feelings of guilt and shame are absolved. This movement from sin acknowledged to forgiveness received is a common spiritual practice. It is a religious action, but it is also profoundly psychological.

Sin, guilt and shame

Psychologists identify guilt and shame as emotions that have developed as part of a useful internal warning system to help us to regulate our behaviour (Tangney and Dearing, 2003; Lewis, 1992; and Brown, 2013 and 2021). From a young age, we experience being told off and temporarily removed: perhaps sent to the naughty step or alone to our rooms for doing something wrong. The telling off and temporary break in connection with a loved parent or caregiver teaches us that we have done something bad; and the negative emotions become connected to the actions. Over time, we begin to learn that there are moral, social and physical boundaries; and when these are crossed, negative things happen. For example, when we grab someone else's toy or hit a sibling, such an action leads to being told off and being temporarily removed from the room, from play and from loved ones.

We learn that when we cross a boundary that should not be crossed or take something that is not ours to take, we may face the social consequence of love being removed and experience the resulting psychological discomfort. Over time, these feelings become internalized and we begin to anticipate the unease before we act. Through this, we learn to notice sensations of discomfort and to monitor and modify our social behaviour to avoid them.

We feel bad about what we did; we have an icky, uncomfortable feeling. We are sorry; we don't want to feel that again; we don't want to do that again. So, we learn that this is a boundary we do not want to cross in future. The uncomfortable feelings act as a helpful warning system to alert us that we are about to cross a boundary we may not want to cross. The warning system may stop us before we cross that boundary or signal when a boundary has started to be crossed, helping us to repair quickly the damage caused. In Christian contexts, this alert system occurs not only with the knowledge of social consequences for actions; it also comes with the belief that God sees all and knows all, withdraws from us when we sin, and comes close and forgives us when we confess.

Psalm 51, frequently used by churches in practices of repentance or in teaching about confession, presents us with numerous vivid images of confession and purification: 'Wash me, cleanse me, purge me and I shall be clean. Wash me, and I shall be whiter than snow.' It vividly captures the raw, disorientating physicality of guilt and shame, and the uneasy emotional weight of it.

FINDING ABSOLUTION

> Have mercy on me, O God,
>   according to your steadfast love;
> according to your abundant mercy
>   blot out my transgressions.
> Wash me thoroughly from my iniquity,
>   and cleanse me from my sin.
>
> For I know my transgressions,
>   and my sin is ever before me.
> Against you, you alone, have I sinned,
>   and done what is evil in your sight,
> so that you are justified in your sentence
>   and blameless when you pass judgement.
> Indeed, I was born guilty,
>   a sinner when my mother conceived me.
>
> You desire truth in the inward being;
>   therefore teach me wisdom in my secret heart.
> Purge me with hyssop, and I shall be clean;
>   wash me, and I shall be whiter than snow.
> Let me hear joy and gladness;
>   let the bones that you have crushed rejoice.
> Hide your face from my sins,
>   and blot out all my iniquities.
> (Psalm 51.1–9)

Arguably, the language employed in Psalm 51 is fitting for the sin committed. This is not a general prayer of confession: it is the confession attributed to King David after he rapes Bathsheba and disposes of her husband.

These images are reminiscent of scenes from crime fiction: the ritual washing of blood off hands and the scrubbing of blood off walls. Washing away the evidence, perhaps, but something more primal is also happening: the instinctive compulsion to remove the stain, to scrub the shame away. There is a deep sense of guilt in the psalm: guilt about the act that was committed. But alongside the guilt lies shame. While guilt is directed at the specific behaviour, '[I have] done what is evil' (v. 4), shame seeps more deeply into the self, 'Indeed, I was born guilty, a sinner when my mother conceived me' (v. 5). The guilt might be resolved through confession or amends but the shame lingers, clinging to identity and self-perception.

Though the terms 'guilt' and 'shame' are tied together in the way we talk about sin, guilt and shame are different emotions, with significantly different outcomes. Unlike guilt, which is closely attached to actions, feelings of shame are connected to the identity of a person. Shame is the feeling of being unworthy of love and belonging. Where guilt says, 'I've done a bad thing,' shame says, 'I am the bad thing' (Brown, 2021, p. 134).

Shame can be felt as an icky, uncomfortable feeling when we do something stupid or embarrassing; or it can be a gut-wrenching, soul-destroying ache when deep psychological boundaries are broken. There is also an intense feeling of wanting to hide, to cover up; not just the mess or the sin, but who we are. As the story goes, Adam and Eve sinned, felt ashamed, saw their nakedness, covered themselves and hid. And we do the same.

Shame, however, can be a confusing emotion because it arises not only from things that we have done, but also from things that have been done to us. While it is understandable to feel shame when we knowingly act against our own values or when we commit sin, we may experience equally intense feelings of shame in response to violations committed against us by others. This is especially true in cases of sexual assault and abuse. Here, the shame does not belong to the survivor, yet it attaches itself to the body and mind as if it does. The victim may internalize the wrong and feel contaminated, exposed or somehow responsible, even when the fault lies entirely with the perpetrator. Whether shame stems from our own actions or from the actions of others, it distorts our sense of self; this leads us to feel not just that something bad has happened, but that we are bad because of it.

FINDING ABSOLUTION

What is happening when we confess?

The congregational practice, from sins confessed to sins absolved, can be understood and experienced in transactional terms within a cycle of exchange and transfer (see Figure 2). For those who repent, sin is taken and exchanged for forgiveness and reconciliation with God.

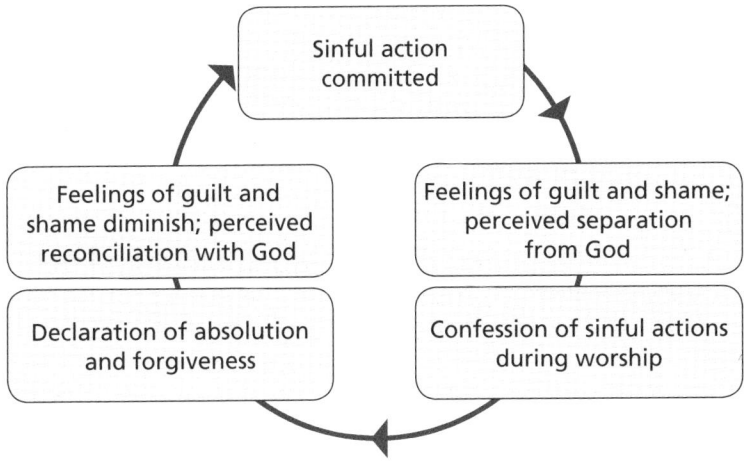

Figure 2: Transactional confession

During the service, worshippers are asked to recall sinful acts they've committed, and to feel the associated guilt and separation from God. Through the act of confession, they receive forgiveness. Negative feelings of guilt and shame diminish, and perceived connection with God is restored. The cycle continues over time through the regular practice of worship; it becomes a normalized route from guilt and separation from God to forgiveness and reconciliation with God.

But this transactional practice does not take account of differences between feelings of guilt for actions committed and more generalized feelings of shame. If Christianity identifies the confession of sin as the route towards forgiveness and peace with

God, where does that leave the victim who is being wrongly blamed, or even scapegoated, for someone else's wrongdoing?

The psychological discomfort felt when someone commits a sin or oversteps a boundary is not unlike the psychological discomfort felt when physical and psychological boundaries are violated by someone else. Here, the victim of someone else's sin experiences similar emotions to the one who has sinned: they feel dirty, ashamed and sad about what happened. Though not responsible, victims report feelings of shame and even of guilt for what happened; they feel that they were somehow complicit or that they should have been able to stop it happening.

In earlier chapters, we explored the intense feelings of shame and self-blame that victims often experience. These feelings of shame and blame may be compounded by the words and actions of close friends and family as they try to come to terms with what has happened. Survivors worshipping in churches influenced by rape-culture assumptions and purity beliefs may experience intensified feelings of shame and rejection from their community and their faith. Survivors may also experience scapegoating. Here, the sins of the perpetrator are explicitly laid on them; and they are asked to carry the shame and the sin committed against them. More than 99 per cent of cases will not lead to a conviction; and those who do report the crime to the police may experience intrusive and victim-blaming questioning. Though victims are in no way responsible for what happened, it's not surprising that they feel a confusing mix of shame and guilt. They can know that it was not their fault and yet feel intense shame about what happened.

In Christian settings, the terms 'sin' and 'shame' have often been bound together. Songs and liturgy often connect them. For example, here is a section from a commonly used prayer in the Church of England:

> we have sinned against you and against our neighbour …
> We are sorry and ashamed,
> and repent of all our sins.
> (From B33, *New Patterns for Worship*, 2016, p. 81)

A sung example could be the second verse of the hymn 'Praise to the Holiest in the Height' by John Henry Newman (1865):

> O loving wisdom of our God!
> When all was sin and shame,
> a second Adam to the fight,
> and to the rescue came.

Or an example from contemporary worship could be the song 'This is our God' by Phil Wickham (2023), which includes the words 'walls that we called sin and shame'. By connecting these words, liturgy, songs and hymns can, unintentionally, communicate and teach that any feelings of shameful discomfort are an emotional symptom of separation from God; that they are caused by sinful actions, whether or not the feelings are the result of guilt from actions committed or shame from violations inflicted by others.

Imagine a person comes to a church with feelings of guilt related to a specific, wrongful action they have committed. The transactional practice of confession enables that person to confess their guilt and then move beyond that to experience forgiveness and reconciliation with God. Their sinful actions and their experience of guilt do not undermine their overall sense of connectedness to God. They are reassured that God forgives all sin; and there is nothing they can do that will separate them from God. Here, the feelings of guilt act as part of the cycle of forgiveness and connection.

Imagine now that a person comes to a church with intense feelings of shame. The feelings are not connected to any sin they have committed but are instead related to having been the victim of abuse or sexual assault. The service begins and soon they are asked, along with the congregation, to engage in confession. They are aware of their feelings of shame; and perhaps even a feeling of guilt because they think they should have been able to stop it happening. In a transactional model of confession and absolution, the way to get rid of these feelings and to feel close to God again is to confess. But here confession makes no sense as there has been little or no choice regarding the sin committed. You cannot confess something you were the victim of; neither can you confess something you had little or no power over.

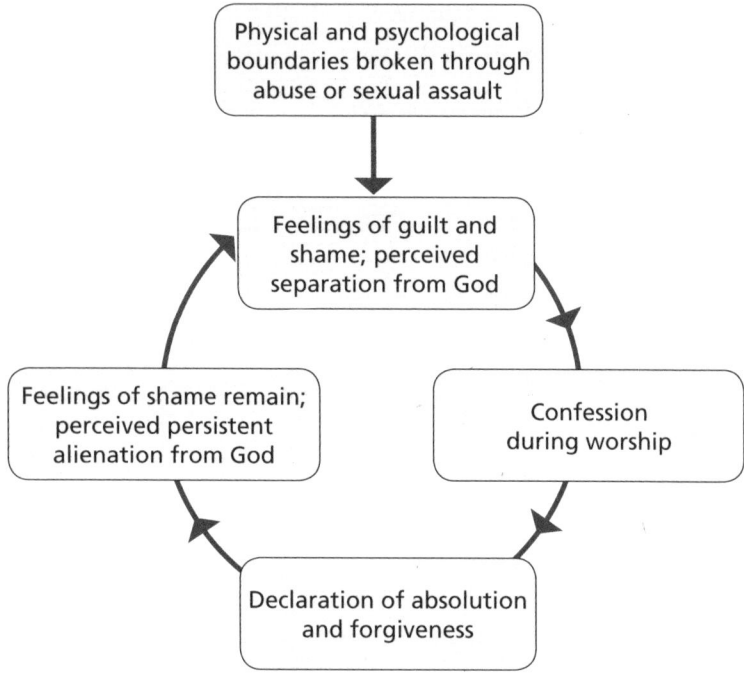

Figure 3: Stuck in the confession loop

In a transactional model of forgiveness, the feelings of shame are identified as the experienced separation between the person and God, which has been caused by sinful acts. Here, feelings of shame are taken as proof of sin, which is resolvable only through confession. So victims are unwittingly encouraged to confess in order to be released from shame and reconciled with God. Absolution and forgiveness are declared over the congregation, but the feelings of shame and guilt do not diminish. A sense of disconnection from God remains; and now there is also a sense of alienation from God and from fellow congregants, who are seemingly experiencing forgiveness, connection and peace with

God. As reconciliation with God is offered essentially through confession, seemingly the only way through this is to re-enter the cycle of confession (see Figure 3).

So, this practice of confession and absolution can unintentionally encourage victims to purge their feelings of shame repeatedly through confession in an attempt to restore connection with God. But as the feelings of shame relate to the actions of others, there is no sin to confess. Survivors are left unable to access the transaction from shame to forgiveness, leaving feelings of shame unresolved and potentially unresolvable. The survivor, after all they have been through, may then perceive that they are separated from God, stuck in a confession loop, perhaps indefinitely. Separated from God who knows all, sees all and will forgive all, if they repent.

Rethinking sin and shame

In Western European contexts, Christian teaching has focused on a transactional view of sin and shame. Here, sin is treated as comprising specific acts, or omissions to act, and shame as the associated feeling. Sins have to be confessed and forgiven for shame to be removed and connection with God restored. This, however, is not the only way Christians have understood sin, shame and reconciliation with God. In cultures where wrongdoing is not bound to Western understandings of sin and shame, ideas about salvation and reconciliation have evolved in different ways. Understandings of shame in East Asian cultures differ greatly from Western understandings; and, here, theologians and missiologists have raised different questions: they ask how shame plays a role in the Gospel narratives and in how people understand salvation. Reconciliation with God is seen less as a transactional model of confession and forgiveness; instead, it is seen as being more focused on restoring relationships, honour and wholeness (You, 1997; Schirrmacher, 2018). More recently in Western European contexts, a fuller understanding of shame has developed from the fields of psychology and therapeutic practice (McClintock, 2011; Campanale, 2021; McNish, 2004) and this has begun to influence theology and ministerial practice (Jamieson, 2016; Rossall, 2020; Nash, 2020).

Reclaiming narratives of restoration

In the Gospels, we see how Jesus responds differently to different people. To those who have been shamed, marginalized or scapegoated, he offers connection and restoration. But he challenges those who have the power to repent and change their ways. Both are a call to walk away from the chaos of sin; both are a call to live anew, recreated through the work of God. But in these Gospel narratives, we see redemption encompassing both forgiveness from sin and liberation from shame.

Jesus met people where they were, but did not leave them unchanged. To those with power, he spoke with clarity and challenge. He called them to examine their lives, to repent not just in words but in action. He asked them to let go of their need for control, to restore what they had taken, to live with integrity. The rich young man was offered a path of freedom through generosity (Matt. 19.16–22). The teachers of the law had their prejudices and hypocrisy confronted (Matthew 23). His words to the powerful were not cruel, but they were uncomfortable: an invitation to live differently, with justice at the centre.

At the same time, Jesus came close to those on the margins and met them with compassion. He touched those who were considered untouchable. He noticed those whom others passed by or thought unclean; those whose lives were marked with physical distress and shame. Whether it was the woman who had been bleeding for many years (Mark 5.25–34) or a leper ostracized by the community (Luke 5.12–13), Jesus gently broke through their shame to offer physical healing and restoration. He confronted the false belief that bad things happen to bad people when he healed the blind man (John 9.1–12) and the paralysed man at the pool (John 5.2–14). Jesus responded differently depending on the circumstance. Whether by challenging or with tenderness, his concern was to restore, set free and embody the kingdom of God.

Prayers of confession and absolution

When we reframe confession beyond a purely transactional model, we move closer to the ways Jesus ministers in the Gospels. This shift helps us to resist patterns of victim blaming and opens us to the range of invitations Jesus offers: the invitation to forgiveness from sin and the invitation to liberation from shame. The language we use in confession matters deeply. It can either reinforce harm or make space for survivors to approach God with honesty and hope.

These two prayers taken from the Church of England Ash Wednesday liturgy illustrate the difference between a transactional model of confession and one that offers space for connection with God.

Prayer A

Almighty and everlasting God,
you hate nothing you have made
and forgive the sins
of all those who are penitent:
create and make in us
new and contrite hearts
that we, worthily lamenting our sins
and acknowledging our wretchedness
may receive from you, the God of all mercy,
perfect remission and forgiveness;
through Jesus Christ your Son our Lord,
who is alive and reigns with you,
in the unity of the Holy Spirit
one God, now and forever.
Amen.

Prayer B

Holy God,
our lives are laid open before you:
rescue us from the chaos of sin
and through the death of your Son
bring us healing and make us whole
in Jesus Christ our Lord.
Amen.
(*Common Worship: Times and Seasons*, 2013, p. 224)

These two prayers differ noticeably in length and tone; they also reveal more subtle theological distinctions. The first reflects a transactional model of confession, where forgiveness is granted only to those who demonstrate penitence, accompanied by a call for worshippers to feel contrite and wretched about their sin. By contrast, the second prayer takes a different approach: it recognizes the chaos and damage caused by sin, without assigning blame; and it pleads for rescue, not on the basis of the worshipper's confession but through the death of Christ. While the first may resonate with those who feel personal guilt over their actions, its emphasis on wretchedness and conditional forgiveness may be troubling for those burdened by chronic shame. The second prayer, by contrast, holds space for both those who have sinned and those who have been wounded by the sins of others; and it seeks deliverance from sin's effects rather than the reinforcement of guilt. Ministers can make choices in the language they use, offering only a transactional approach to confession or adapting to more comprehensive understandings of trauma-related shame. The choices they make can have the effect of opening or shutting down routes for connection with God.

8

Forgiveness

Forgive us our sins as we forgive those who sin against us.

I usually say these words at least once every day. They come up in daily prayer and in most services I conduct. They are familiar words that trip off the tongue. But they are also hard words, sometimes difficult to say. Sometimes, I glide over them, knowing they will still be here when I want to return and give them my full attention. Sometimes they stick at the back of my throat, like a shard of glass cutting into my flesh. Sometimes, they chase around my mind, looking for some kind of resolution; but finding none, they keep chasing, until I am too tired to think any more. They lurk in hidden corners, ready to start up their search again tomorrow.

Separating justice and forgiveness

So, let's be clear, because sometimes the Church has confused this: justice and forgiveness are entirely different things. Violence, assault and abuse are not personal or private issues: they are crimes. They are crimes against the victim and also crimes against the community. The adjudication of crime belongs in the courtroom, not in the confessional. Given that we have such low rates of conviction – and the fact that many victims do not even report their experiences, having lost trust in policing and systems of justice – means we need to do so much more to bring justice for victims and to make our communities safer.

Crime is a public order issue and should be judged in public.

Too often, the Church has blurred this, urging victims to forgive instead of seeking justice: turning forgiveness into a tool to preserve reputation. Whatever your take on the principles behind our systems of justice, conflating justice and forgiveness cannot offer any reasonable answers, as they are entirely different processes.

The shape of forgiveness

It's hard to talk about forgiveness without sounding glib. Sermons rarely do it justice; and I have found listening to victims talk about forgiveness much more convincing than any sermonizing on the subject. Forgiveness is deeply personal and often private. Forgiveness cannot be required, demanded or even encouraged from victims. This is especially the case for crimes of sexual violence, which defile and dehumanize. Those who have lost so much, and yet can speak about that loss with dignity, have something rare and precious to share; and I am all ears for that.

As a survivor, I have found forgiveness hard. But it has also been an important part of my path, part of my walking on from my experiences: a path that has been made so much harder each time I have seen church leaders bang on about forgiveness, while protecting perpetrators, silencing victims and placing reputation above truth. In this chapter, I want to explore what forgiveness might be, how it functions and whether it has limits.

We are, all of us, creatures of need and longing. We so readily trespass into one another's lives and leave damage behind. Some wounds are accidental, others deliberate; and many unfold in the grey spaces between intention and impact. We take others for granted and sometimes take things that were never ours to take. Sometimes, what is taken can be quantified. Sometimes, what is taken cannot be named so easily: an image of the self before the harm; a future that once felt possible; the sense of being held or safe in the world. Not all harm is visible; not all loss is recognized. We instinctively react to being hurt in different ways. Some retreat inside themselves, locking the hurt into silence. Others become vengeful and angry. Others numb the pain.

Forgiveness doesn't come in one fixed form. It arrives differently for each of us: sometimes quietly, sometimes all at once, sometimes not at all. It can be hard to name, even harder to hold. Just when you think you've found it, it can shift or slip away again.

- Forgiveness is hard when there seems no reason or rationale behind the pain caused.
- Forgiveness is hard when the misconduct is not acknowledged or is even denied.
- Forgiveness is hard when there seems to be no justice.
- Forgiveness is hard when there is no apology.
- Forgiveness is hard when the action is covered up or lied about.
- Forgiveness cannot be coerced, prescribed, demanded or pushed as a duty.
- Forgiveness is a gift, freely given.

Forgiveness seems to be good for us. Research shows that people who forgive tend to score higher on just about every measure of psychological well-being. Whereas lack of forgiveness appears to prolong stress and other aspects of physical ill health (Toussaint, Owen and Cheadle, 2012). But the motivations behind forgiveness can vary widely. Some people talk of wanting to end the cycle of hate. Others want to focus on using their suffering to shed light on wider injustices in society. Some seek restored relationship. Others choose forgiveness as a way of reclaiming power or a sense of control. And some seek meaning in the mess or simply want to let go, transforming the pain to move beyond it.

Forgiveness may be good for us, but it's also really weird. Masi Noor and Marina Cantacuzino's book, *Forgiveness Is Really Strange* (2018), explores how odd forgiveness can be. How strange is it that one way of coping with loss is to give something precious, our forgiveness, to the very person who was caught robbing us? How strange is it that sometimes someone's instinctive reaction to an act of violence or extreme loss is to offer almost spontaneous forgiveness? How strange is it that some people commit to a conscious decision to live in forgiveness in the face of ongoing injustice? Forgiveness may break the cycle of revenge, but it doesn't mean it removes the pain. Today, you could forgive and tomorrow feel the pain all over again. And here forgiveness lies: somewhere between the chaos of loss and the desire for order that gives meaning to our lives. Sometimes, we desperately want to forgive, but we're stuck. We might believe in forgiveness, value it, even admire it in others, but still find it unreachable.

Does forgiveness have limits?

Some suggest there should be no limit to forgiveness, perhaps even quoting Jesus' response to Peter in Matthew 18.

> 'Lord, if another member of the church sins against me, how often should I forgive? As many as seven times?' Jesus said to him, 'Not seven times, but, I tell you, seventy-seven times.' (Matt. 18.21–22)

In his book *Unforgivable? Exploring the Limits of Forgiveness*, Stephen Cherry questions the Christian teaching that there are no limits to forgiveness. He is highly critical of what happens when the Church pushes forgiveness too quickly, too neatly, especially in response to deep and lasting harm. He names the problems that arise when forgiveness becomes a test of faith or a shortcut to restoring order. Well-meaning calls to forgive and move on can end up placing a fresh burden on the wounded rather than on those who caused the harm. The result is a spiritual sleight of hand, where the responsibility quietly shifts from the perpetrator to the survivor.

Cherry highlights several places where this distortion creeps in. An example of this is where Jesus' words from the Cross, 'Father, forgive them', are used as a blanket instruction, rather than a prayer. He writes:

FORGIVENESS

It was a prayer. It was directed at God. It wasn't an act of forgiveness … Jesus didn't offer forgiveness from the cross, and he certainly didn't command anyone to forgive from that unlikely pulpit. It is one of the several myths that have grown up and which exaggerate the importance that forgiving has in Christianity … there really are limits to the possibilities of forgiveness of every human being, and recognizing these limits is fundamentally important to respecting and supporting those who have been harmed … It is the Christ on the cross, who registers the need for forgiveness and does not achieve it or deliver it, who can save them … [In saying] 'Father forgive,' and not 'I forgive,' Jesus opened a positive path for all who have suffered the unforgivable and proved that he was the Saviour of the abused, the exploited and the oppressed. (Cherry, 2024, pp. 121–3)

Cherry is critical of how stories of reconciliation, like that of the prodigal son, are retold in superficial ways, without any need for truth-telling or repair – as if a hug were enough to restore what was lost. Public narratives of dramatic, almost heroic forgiveness are held up as the gold standard, implying that if you're still angry, still hurt, still struggling to forgive, you're somehow doing it wrong.

Cherry offers instead non-vengeful unforgiveness as a more faithful route for victims: a way of saying, 'I will not harm you, but I will not release you from responsibility either.' It holds open a third space: not vengeance, not forgiveness; but a refusal to excuse harm that gives survivors moral space to breathe.

Forgiveness, if and when it comes, must be real. It must be chosen. It cannot be demanded and it certainly cannot be used to measure someone's progress or faith. He reframes forgiveness not as a duty, but as something that might possibly grow in the soil of justice and repentance. And if it doesn't grow, that is not a failure. There is something deeply pastoral in this. Cherry's theology holds space for lament; for anger; for slowness; for silence. In this way, Cherry helps survivors to hold on to the possibility that even in unforgiveness there can still be holiness; that not forgiving may be the most truthful response to harm.

No script for forgiveness

My own journey towards forgiveness started with rage; not the clean kind of anger you can channel into something useful. This was raw, exhausting and disorienting rage: rage at what had been done to me; at what had been stolen; at the long shadow of consequences that stretched far beyond the violence itself. Life didn't just change in that moment: it kept changing; unravelling in ways I couldn't predict, let alone control. And I was left stumbling through it, trying to keep up with the aftershocks.

Then there was the anger that followed me long after others thought the story was over: anger about the silence; about the people who looked the other way or crossed to the other side of the road; about the way life became fractured, not just for a moment, but for years. It seeped into everything.

My brain wouldn't stop. It spun continuously, looping through what had happened, what should have happened, what might have been. I was trying to process it; to understand it; to make it make sense. But no sense would come. The best way I can describe it is like the low hum of a computer fan, always running in the background; occasionally kicking up into overdrive when the heat of emotion or memory pushed it too far.

I knew the theology. I'd read the verses. I knew Jesus said to forgive 'seventy times seven'. I'd prayed the words countless times: 'Forgive us our sins as we forgive those who sin against us.' But those words didn't feel like a roadmap. They felt like a riddle.

I needed stories; not parables or theological arguments, but real stories from real people. I looked to Jesus; but, honestly, that just felt ridiculous. I'm not God. Perhaps forgiveness is divine work, something that, really, only God can do. But then where does that leave the rest of us?

I needed something more human. So, I started looking for stories from people like me: people who had lived through loss; people who had wrestled with forgiveness, not in abstract but in blood and bone and breath. I wanted to hear from people who had faced worse and still found a way. I needed to know it was possible – not easy, not tidy, but possible.

In those stories, I started to find fragments, glimpses of something real. People who had lost whole parts of themselves. People who weren't preaching but were telling the truth about the long, slow, painful road they'd walked.

Some of those stories came from The Forgiveness Project, a charity that collects the personal testimonies of people who've lived through trauma and chosen, in some way, to forgive (see Figure 4). Not everyone featured has found forgiveness. Some are still in the process. Some have chosen other routes. But all of them speak with rawness and dignity about what it means to live after harm. The stories come from all backgrounds, all faiths and none. And they're not romantic. They're real. They acknowledge that forgiveness, if it comes at all, does so differently for everyone. There is no script; no universal timeline; no right way to do it.

Figure 4: The F Word exhibition from The Forgiveness Project at St Mark's Church, Broomhill, Sheffield, June 2020

Reading those stories helped. They didn't solve anything; but they kept me company. Another companion on this journey was Marian Partington. I came across her book *If You Sit Very Still* (2012); and slowly, over the course of a year, I meticulously read it. Marian's sister, Lucy, was one of the victims of Fred and Rosemary West. It's an almost unimaginable story and the book is difficult to read. I know suffering isn't something you can line up and measure; you can't make comparisons. But still, in some kind of rational sense, I knew she had much more to forgive than me. And so I found myself drawn to her; not to compare wounds, but because she seemed to be someone I could follow: someone who could challenge me; someone I couldn't turn my back on.

Her book is raw, quiet and poetic, deeply spiritual; rooted in stillness and fierce honesty. She doesn't clean the story up. She lets the mess remain visible and, in that, she offers something true. She didn't rush to forgive. She lived with the weight of it all. She wept. She raged. She wandered through years of grief and numbness. But slowly, she began to find words, not to fix it but to name it, to hold it and to let some light in.

In one section (p. 65), Marian recalls a quote, stuck on her fridge, something a bereaved mother once told her:

Forgiveness means giving up all hope of a better past.

I read that line and felt my body tighten. Everything in me wanted to argue against it. Surely forgiveness didn't mean accepting the unacceptable. Surely knowing something was wrong could and should mean believing the past should have been different. Surely I could rage against the past and still reach towards something more redemptive in the future? Couldn't I forgive and still believe and hope that the past should have been different?

Confused, I looked about for some corroboration. I found my husband (who happens to be a psychotherapist), standing at the kitchen sink.

'Do you think this is a good description of forgiveness?' I tried to sound as neutral as I could while I read from the book. 'Forgiveness means giving up all hope of a better past.'

He barely looked up from the dishes. 'Yeah,' he said gently. 'That sounds about right.'

It felt more than a little ironic: me, a priest, standing up week after week to proclaim forgiveness and speak words of absolution, floundering around in my own tangled questions about what forgiveness is. It seemed embarrassingly late in the day to be wrestling with one of the basics of the Christian faith. But the more I sat with it, the more bewildered I became. If forgiveness did mean giving up all hope of a better past, then I wasn't sure I wanted it at all.

I kept going. I kept turning up; kept praying the prayers, saying the words I'd said a thousand times before. 'Forgive us our sins ...' I said it aloud on behalf of others, even when I wasn't sure what it meant for me. But the real collision came at the altar. Each time I lifted the bread and said, 'This is my body, given for you,' it landed with unexpected force. Words that were supposed to reassure, to anchor the congregation in grace, seemed an echo of my inner storm. The words flared like a raw nerve, mirroring the fracture I carried inside and the forgiveness I still couldn't find.

Embodied

Trauma is not simply remembered but felt, flashing through the nervous system, tightening the breath, bracing the muscles. In a similar way, forgiveness, after trauma, is woven through the body as much as the mind. You can think about whether something was wrong (it was) and whether it should have been different (it should), and that you want to set that aside and move on. Yet, the ache still pulses in the gut; the shoulders still rise; the jaw still locks. No amount of mental calculation can untangle that; no matter how many times you say to yourself, 'I should forgive. I want to forgive.' Perhaps this is what Stephen Cherry gestures towards with his idea of non-vengeful unforgiveness. It holds two truths at once: 'What happened is unforgivable' and 'I will not seek revenge'. Perhaps it mirrors Jesus' prayer 'Father, forgive', for I know I cannot. It respects the body's honest recoil from harm while refusing to add fresh harm in return.

Over time, as therapy, rest, prayer and community help the nervous system breathe again, the body may begin to loosen its grip. Muscles unclench, the heart rate steadies, new memories find space alongside the old. In those moments, the body itself practises a kind of forgiveness: forgiveness of the self and forgiveness of the past, even before the mind has fully made sense of it. Allowing survivors space to name what was unforgivable, and allowing the possibility that it will always remain so, may provide the space needed for the embodied work of recovery.

Jesus spoke about forgiveness. But louder than his words, through his own body, I find meaning and understanding about what forgiveness can be; not in explanation or demand or reason, but in person: in the dying and living Jesus. As tragedy moves close, Jesus moves further into connection with others. There is so much that distracts and distorts; that pulls me away from my connectedness to God. I do not want to hear a holier-than-thou attitude; a demand that I forgive, or forget, or move on, or ignore, or pretend it did not happen. No words can explain away the pain of loss or answer for the injustice. But here I can see Jesus. I see how love persists and braves the horror of broken bodies; that, somehow, beauty can be found beyond loss and betrayal. This seems to be the work of God: God with us, broken and yet living; present in our suffering, present in our healing.

In Jesus, we meet God who stands in solidarity with the wounded; and we encounter one who carves out a path through the wreckage. Jesus doesn't bypass the horror or sanitize the truth. He bears it in his body. He does not flinch from the reality of what broken bodies endure. And yet, from within that place, a path emerges: a path that survivors can walk at their own pace, without pressure or pretence; a path that doesn't demand forgiveness as a condition but offers life as a possibility.

This is not a path of easy restoration, where things are put neatly back as they were. It is a path shaped by scars, by rips, by tears and loose ends. In Christ's body, we glimpse what it means to survive with God: to resurrect. The journey from abuse to life

FORGIVENESS

is not one of forgetting or pretending, but of being accompanied on a path that has been trod before. It is not the body dragged toward forgiveness by force of will; but the body held in love, in safety and released from harm. This way is a path on which truth is told, pain is held and life is made possible again.

9

Repair

In 2023, Judith Herman published her long-awaited follow-up to *Trauma and Recovery*. It was titled *Truth and Repair: How Trauma Survivors Envision Justice*. Many had high hopes for this second volume. Herman's first book had changed the landscape, offering not only language but also legitimacy to what survivors had long known about trauma's impact. It gave clarity, theory, even solidarity. So, it was perhaps inevitable that her new book would be met with longing: for resolution, for answers, for something that might tidy the mess of recovery and offer a path to justice.

Truth and Repair does not tidy things up. It does not offer a grand solution. It offers something more honest but difficult: a return to the long, unfinished work of justice. For some in the survivor community, there was disappointment – not because the book failed to name reality, but because it named, again, how complex and slow this work really is. Herman does not propose a new system that will finally bring justice. Instead, she amplifies the voices of survivors who know only too well that justice, as it stands, often fails them. The criminal justice system does not offer healing. It rarely offers justice in any meaningful sense. Survivors must, once again, find ways to navigate a broken system and, when that fails, must begin the even harder work of imagining repair outside of it.

The legal system is not built to meet the needs of those who have been sexually violated. It is adversarial, retraumatizing and often shaped more by myth and prejudice than truth. Conviction rates remain low. Cross-examination becomes a theatre of humiliation. Survivors are expected to be calm, coherent, perfect witnesses of their own pain. Herman writes that although survivors are often stereotyped as vengeful, survivors' needs are not primarily about punishment. Their vision of justice tends to be centred less on vengeance than on truth and prevention.

Many survivors feel very ambivalent about punishment because it does nothing substantive to repair the harm that has been done to them. Rather, they try to envisage alternatives that would require the perpetrator and complicit bystanders to make amends. What might it mean to hold perpetrators accountable for repairing the harm they have done? What might it mean to hold bystanders accountable for acts of complicity and collusion? What about acts of omission, indifference or wilful blindness? These are the questions that survivors grapple with as they try to define a new idea of justice (Herman, 2023, pp. 109–10).

Survivors need space to speak, to name what happened, without being discredited, silenced or blamed. Understandably, the justice system tends to treat truth as something that must be proved, measured against legal criteria and tested under pressure. But survivors' truths are often messy, embodied, partial and disrupted by trauma. They do not always fit courtroom narratives. Still, their stories must be heard; not only for their own sake, but because public acknowledgement of harm is the first step towards any moral reckoning.

Justice is not only legal but also political and moral. When survivors are disbelieved or dismissed, it reflects broader systems of power that protect the powerful and silence the vulnerable. Justice, in this sense, is about truth, yes, but it is also about who is permitted to speak; who is recognized as harmed; who is allowed to be angry.

Herman's vision of justice is a move towards repair: repair in the sense not of undoing or fixing the past but of moral repair. It is a form of accountability that acknowledges the wrong, takes responsibility (pp. 109–41) and works towards restitution (pp. 145–65). This might look like apology; like financial compensation; like community transformation or systemic reform. It is grounded in what survivors want; not in what institutions are willing to offer.

Repair is not a soft alternative to punishment. It is a deeper, harder work because it requires the courage to listen, to change, to be changed. Repair is not the survivor's responsibility alone. Recovery cannot be privatized or placed as another burden on the survivor to fix. It requires a collective response. Churches, communities and institutions must reckon with their complicity, their silence, their failure to act. They must take up the work of prevention, not only by setting safeguarding policies but by transforming the cultures that enabled harm in the first place (Herman, 2023, pp. 191–220).

What Herman offers is not a blueprint for simple justice; instead, it is one shaped by survivors' wisdom, rooted in truth-telling and oriented towards communal repair. It is, in many ways, a refusal to settle for what currently exists; and we are invited to imagine something more relational, more honest and more human. This invitation is profoundly relevant to the Church. We cannot rely on the legal system alone to enact justice, nor can we expect survivors to carry the burden of repair. If we are to be part of this moral work, we must be willing to listen, to act and to be changed.

Practising repair

The Church must choose what kind of community it wants to be. A place that listens without demanding. A place that names harm, even when it implicates those in power. A place where justice begins with truth and where recovery is not confused with silencing. Churches are not powerless in the face of harm. There are practical steps and meaningful actions they can take to respond with care, integrity and accountability. By choosing to engage in practices of repair, churches can become places where recovery is made possible, and justice begins to take root. Such commitment requires the courage to accept uncomfortable truths and to resist the temptation to protect institutions over individuals. By doing this, the Church not only proclaims redemption but actively participates in its unfolding.

REPAIR

1 Respond well when someone discloses

Most survivors decide within the first few minutes whether it is safe to keep talking, so how you respond really matters. Each church denomination should have a safeguarding policy on how to respond to a disclosure. All ministers and members of governing bodies, staff and volunteers have a duty to follow these steps. Policies such as these safeguard against the well-meaning amateur who asks probing questions, doubts a timeline or promises confidentiality they cannot keep.

When someone discloses abuse, it is important to listen attentively and without interruption, allowing the person to speak in their own words. It's important not to interrogate or investigate, but simply to receive what is offered with compassion. The person should be gently reassured that they have done the right thing in coming forward, while being told honestly that their disclosure cannot be kept entirely confidential: it will have to be shared with someone who can help. The details should be recorded as soon as possible, using the individual's own words wherever possible, while avoiding speculation or interpretation. The concern must be referred promptly to the safeguarding officer; never handled alone or informally.

Alongside this process, it is important to consider the person's immediate safety and well-being. If they are at risk of ongoing harm or in immediate danger, steps should be taken to help them to a safe place or to access emergency support from the police or medical professionals. Even when there is no imminent risk, pastoral care remains essential. The church's role is not to rush towards resolution but to provide calm, grounded support, respecting the person's agency and pace. Signposting to therapeutic or specialist services may be appropriate. A safeguarding response must always prioritize the survivor's safety and dignity, not the protection of the institution. The way a disclosure is handled can support a victim toward recovery or deepen the harm already done. Churches should resist the urge to handle things alone and instead connect survivors with the professional support they need. This includes encouraging access to Independent

Sexual Violence Advisors (ISVAs), trauma-informed counsellors, sexual-assault referral centres and the police. The Church's responsibility is not to act as a substitute for professional care: it is to walk alongside survivors as they access care; to create pathways, not roadblocks, to repair and justice.

2 *Survivor-led support*

It is vital that our support for victims and survivors is shaped by their needs, not by the needs of institutions or our own desire to feel helpful. Too often, responses to harm are managed on the terms of the institution, which may prioritize reputation, risk management or timelines that serve organizational convenience. But genuine care begins by listening and by centring the experience, voice and autonomy of those who have been harmed. This means resisting the urge to control or define what recovery should look like; and instead allowing survivors to lead the way, trusting their insight into what safety, justice and support mean for them. By doing so, we begin to create spaces where repair is possible and dignity is restored.

3 *Foster a safeguarding culture and recognize the signs of spiritual abuse*

Safeguarding should never be a subsidiary task delegated to one overstretched officer. It is the atmosphere a healthy church breathes; woven into the fabric of how we worship, plan, care and lead. A safeguarding culture is built when every rota, small group, service and PCC agenda quietly asks, 'Does this make people, especially the vulnerable, more safe or less safe?' Safeguarding training has to be expected, revisited and taken seriously. It is not a tick-box exercise but a shared responsibility that shapes how we live together as a community of care.

Essential to this culture is learning to recognize spiritually abusive uses of Scripture, prayer, authority or discipline, to control, coerce or shame others. Identifying spiritual abuse is not always clear cut and can begin with behaviours that feel unhealthy. Survivors often describe these dynamics long before any physical harm is disclosed. By naming and discussing spiritual abuse openly, we strip away its power to operate unnoticed in the shadow of authority. Churches must be places where power is held accountable and where people are free not only to belong but to speak and question without fear.

4 Speak the truth

Truth-telling is the beginning of justice. It means naming what happened, acknowledging what was covered up and repenting for the harm caused, not only by perpetrators but by the systems that enabled them. It means saying, 'This was abuse. This was wrong. You were failed. You are believed.'

5 Let go of the fear of anger

Survivors' anger is not something to fear or suppress. It is not a sign of spiritual failure or emotional instability. Anger, when it arises from the wounds of abuse, is often a deeply sacred response; it signals that something profoundly wrong has taken place. It points to a breach of justice, a betrayal of trust, a failure of protection. It is not the enemy of healing but often the voice of truth breaking through silence.

Churches must learn to witness this anger without defensiveness. Too often, survivors are expected to speak with politeness, patience or theological clarity in order to be heard. But this expectation of perfection places yet another burden on those already carrying too much. People who have been harmed may speak with grief, with rage or with pain that cannot be neatly packaged; and that is OK. Their humanity must be received in all its rawness. They do not owe us composure.

The task of leaders, especially, is to resist the impulse to control or contain anger. We must stop rushing to defend institutions, to correct tone or to explain things away. Anger does not need to be fixed, silenced or prayed away: it needs to be honoured. It needs to be heard, without being edited or diminished. To listen with humility and care is not weakness.

When we disengage from anger, or retreat behind institutional caution, we do not remain neutral: we deepen the harm. But when we choose instead to stay present, to listen, to acknowledge what has been done and what has been broken, we begin to create space where repair might take root.

6 Confront purity teaching and rape culture

Purity culture frames sexual worthiness as a commodity that can be spoiled, reinforcing the logic that a survivor is *damaged goods*. Rape culture in wider society tells similar lies in secular language. Churches must challenge both. That starts by preaching the difficult passages instead of skipping them, naming victims in the text and challenging the power dynamics at play. When people hear these texts unpacked honestly, myths about consent and modesty begin to lose their grip.

Review how prayer ministry happens: what is being said and prayed over people? Do these mirror purity myths or challenge them? Swap sermon illustrations that joke about *boys being boys* for stories that honour bodily autonomy.

Invite speakers from local rape crisis centres to Sunday forums. Update youth-group curricula to include explicit teaching on consent, pornography and coercion. The goal is a congregation equipped to spot cultural lies and committed to living a different story.

7 Review your theology and ask honestly, 'Could this do harm?'

Victim blaming flourishes wherever sermons and liturgies blur shame and sin into a single, undifferentiated burden. When worship implies that every feeling of shame must be proof of personal guilt, survivors are nudged – sometimes overtly, sometimes by implication – into endless cycles of confession for crimes committed against them. True pastoral care resists that collapse. It distinguishes wrongdoing (which calls for repentance) from wounding (which calls for restoration). Prayers and preaching need the same clarity: naming sin without equating it with the visceral shame that abusers so often impose on their victims.

The Church must tread with care when she speaks of crucifixion. Survivors are listening. If our language suggests that pain is pleasing to God or that suffering must be silently endured for some greater good, we risk retraumatizing those who have already borne too much. The Cross is not a divine ledger demanding satisfaction, but God's act of ultimate solidarity with the violated. Preach it as a site where systemic violence is exposed and judged, not as an episode of holy child abuse. Listen again to your sermons: could any phrase be heard that way? If so, reframe it to emphasize God's refusal to let violence have the last word.

It's good to review and question our worship practices. What happens when we sing hymns and songs based on Psalm 51, David's confession after committing abuse? When we set David's words of confession to music, especially in contexts of healing or invitation, have we fully considered how they might be heard by those who carry the wounds of similar harm? It is not that texts like this have no place, but that their use requires deep thought and pastoral sensitivity. Before we choose them, we must pause and ask: what message does this send about whose voices we centre and whose pain we may inadvertently overlook? Is it ever appropriate to use the confession of a rapist as a general call to repentance? And if it does not feel comfortable in that worship setting to name the background to the confession, arguably it is not appropriate to use those words, however poetic they are.

Good Friday poses a similar challenge. Its language of sacrifice, blood and obedience can mirror the logic of abuse if left unexamined. Yet, handled with care, the Passion narrative can become a powerful moment of solidarity; a truth-telling place: one where survivors are neither invisible nor asked to sanctify harm. Rather, they are invited to recognize a companion in Christ, who has walked the same road. 'The body of Christ, broken for you' can echo with anguish; but small shifts in our language can make a vast pastoral difference. 'The body of Christ, which violence could not silence.' Here, harm is acknowledged, yet agency and resurrection are affirmed; naming trauma aloud allows survivors to inhabit worship without disowning their story. Avoid statements that portray suffering as intrinsically holy or redemptive. Affirm instead messages of a God who meets us in suffering but does not require it.

Reviewing the ways we speak about God is not an academic exercise but a pastoral imperative. Our task is not to explain suffering away or to extract redemptive meaning from another's wounds. It is to stand beside those who suffer, name abuse truthfully and insist that violence is never holy and love never demands it.

8 Root out victim blaming and scapegoating

Victim blaming and scapegoating continue to cause profound harm in our churches. We have seen how these patterns play out in Scripture: with Job's friends, who moralize his suffering; and with the woman dragged before Jesus, in John 8, to be used and discarded. These stories are not distant: they are mirrors. The Church should learn to recognize when these dynamics surface in real time: when survivors are doubted; when questions are silenced; when one person is isolated to protect the comfort of the many.

This is not just about theology: it's about culture. We must train ourselves, and our congregations, to spot victim-blaming language when it creeps in: the subtle tone that asks, 'What did they do wrong?' or the impulse to make someone's pain a problem to be removed. We must challenge scapegoating wherever it hides, especially when the one raising the alarm becomes the one pushed out. Churches committed to justice will refuse to sacrifice the vulnerable in order to preserve appearances. They will tell the truth, even when it is costly, and stand by those at risk of being scapegoated.

9 Choose solidarity, not withdrawal

A survivor's journey is rarely short or simple. While churches may offer care during the immediate aftermath of a disclosure, many quietly step back once the crisis moment passes, worried about saying the wrong thing, picking at wounds or reopening pain. But true solidarity does not retreat when things become uncomfortable. It stays the course. It means checking in not just for weeks but for months, even years. It means showing up in court if a case goes to trial. It means offering lifts to therapy, help with childcare or simply texting to say, 'I'm still here.' When we don't know what to say, it is worth remembering that a gentle presence rarely harms, but silence and withdrawal almost always do.

Solidarity also means speaking out. Churches carry moral and institutional weight, and they must use it. Write to MPs about court delays and legal reform. Host prayer vigils as part of the UN's 16 Days of Activism against Gender-Based Violence (from 25 November to 10 December each year). Join campaigns demanding better services for survivors. Public acts of advocacy are not just symbolic. They send a clear message: 'We believe you. You are not alone. We have not moved on.'

This is not the work of quick fixes but of long, patient accompaniment. Solidarity means making space for grief and lament in our liturgies, not rushing people toward healing. It includes financial and practical support; not as charity but as a recognition that many survivors have been left to carry impossible burdens alone. It means investing in theological education for ministers, resources for congregations and proper support for those brave enough to speak out.

Ultimately, the Church must choose solidarity over self-preservation. There will be a cost to truth-telling. Institutions may be shaken. Leaders may fall. Reputations may suffer. But if the Church longs for resurrection, it must be willing to pass through the Cross: not as a passive acceptance of suffering, but as an active dismantling of injustice.

10 *Allow forgiveness to grow hand in hand with recovery*

Forgiveness, if it comes, must arise freely from within the survivor. It cannot be forced, expected or used as a measure of spiritual maturity. Too often, the Church has treated forgiveness as a fast-track solution to healing or reconciliation, as though it were a required step before someone can truly belong again, be believed or be welcomed back into community. But forgiveness is not a condition for faithfulness. It is not a litmus test for wholeness. It is, at best, a fruit that may grow slowly over time.

The process of forgiveness is not linear. It is not a single decision made in the mind: it is something that lives in the body, in the nervous system, in the places where trauma has taken hold. Even if a person desires to forgive, their body may still be gripped by the ache of betrayal or the sharp reflex of fear. Forgiveness may take years. It may arrive quietly. Or it may never feel possible. None of these realities makes a survivor less faithful or less spiritual. Churches must learn to honour this truth: to honour survivors who say, 'I am not ready. I may never be.' Churches must learn to understand that this is not bitterness: it is integrity and the refusal to bypass the real work of recovery with a pseudo-spiritual shortcut. When forgiveness is demanded too soon, it becomes a silencing tool. It protects the institution or the perpetrator rather than the person who has been harmed. It shuts down the anger, grief and disruption that are necessary for healing and justice to unfold.

11 *Support redress*

Money cannot undo trauma. But lack of money can stop recovery in its tracks. Survivors often carry not only emotional and physical scars but also financial burdens: a missed education, disrupted careers, therapy costs, legal fees. Redress is not about paying for pain: it is about recognizing the very real cost of what has been taken and choosing to respond with tangible care. Handled well, emergency grants, access to professional counselling and longer-term redress schemes are all ways the Church can begin to take responsibility for its past and invest in a survivor's future.

Redress is more than financial compensation. It is a moral and pastoral response: a form of public acknowledgement that harm occurred; that the Church failed to protect; and that restitution, however limited, is necessary. Survivors have asked for this for decades. When redress is offered voluntarily, it sends a powerful message that victims matter more than our fear, our funds or our reputation.

The Church of England has begun the journey towards offering such redress through its developing Redress Scheme. While imperfect and still unfolding, it is a crucial step. Other churches and denominations have not yet established formal schemes, but that does not mean they cannot begin. Local churches can advocate for denominational accountability, fund survivor support directly or contribute to independent charities already doing this work.

Supporting redress is not an optional extra. It is a sign that the Church is willing to match its words with action and to shoulder, even in part, the weight of the harm it has caused.

The costly discipleship of repair

Supporting survivors is not just a pastoral task, it is a gospel-shaped calling rooted in justice, generosity and repair. Like Zacchaeus, who felt convicted to give back what he had taken and more, the Church is called to face its own past honestly. Some parishes and institutions carry debts that are not only financial but also relational and moral, owed to those who have been harmed, silenced or driven away. Like Zacchaeus, we are not called to wallow in guilt but to allow our encounter with Christ to transform us; to open our hands; to restore what was lost; and to begin the slow, costly work of repair. It is not enough to apologize with words: restitution is an act of discipleship.

And like the good Samaritan, the Church is called to respond to what is right in front of us: not just when it is convenient or safe, but even when the path is risky; when it means crossing boundaries, disrupting routines and tending to wounds that others have walked past. The Samaritan didn't simply offer a prayer and move on. He stopped. He bound wounds. He made space. He carried the man to safety and ensured his ongoing care. This is what it means to support survivors: to see them, to stop, to listen, to offer practical and continuing support – not just for the crisis moment but also for the long journey of recovery.

In the early Church, we see a community shaped by the teachings of Jesus and formed by putting these teachings into action. When some were being overlooked and excluded, the Church appointed deacons to make sure they were seen and fed. When needs arose, people shared their wealth, laying it at the apostles' feet to be redistributed, so that no one went without. This is not abstract idealism – it is the radical practicality of love in action. A church that cares for survivors must be willing to structure itself around that same justice and generosity: to raise and release funds for therapeutic support; to create safe processes for disclosure; to build cultures that believe, protect and restore.

Maybe, like Zacchaeus, you represent a church or an institution with debts to pay. Maybe, like the Samaritan, you are the one who sees the pain in front of you and has a choice to walk on or to respond. Either way, the invitation is to participate. The Church cannot undo what has been done. But it can decide what kind of community it will be now: one that turns away or one that stays and stands in solidarity; one that protects power or one that makes space for those who've been harmed. The choice is ours.

10

The Pieces Join

In 2017, when I was working at Sheffield Cathedral, I was invited, alongside my friend Neil Marchant, to help to develop a series of prayer installations for the cathedral's Lost and Found exhibition. This was a creative project that ran from Easter to Pentecost, designed to explore Christian themes through art and reflection. As we began to plan, Neil and I found ourselves drawn to something tactile, something communal, something rooted in ordinary life.

The inspiration came from local folk and craft traditions: those found in working communities across South Yorkshire. In past generations, families would gather up old clothes – torn shirts, worn dresses – and bits of fabric long past their use, and patiently thread them through hessian sacks to create rag rugs. These were often made as wedding gifts or for special occasions. They were acts of love and care, stitched together from scraps. The beauty came not from perfection, but from the very ordinariness of the materials and the use of something old and torn to make something precious. The idea began to take shape. We called it the Rag Cross.

It became a city-wide project, involving schools and churches across Sheffield. In the weeks leading up to Easter, willow cross frames were distributed to schools; clergy were invited to visit classrooms to talk about the themes of Holy Week and Easter, of loss, and death and resurrection. Then, together with the children, they began to weave wool and strips of cloth into the willow frames (see Figure 5). Each scrap represented a prayer, a thought or simply a moment of participation. Children were encouraged to bring their own material from home: old fabric,

THE PIECES JOIN

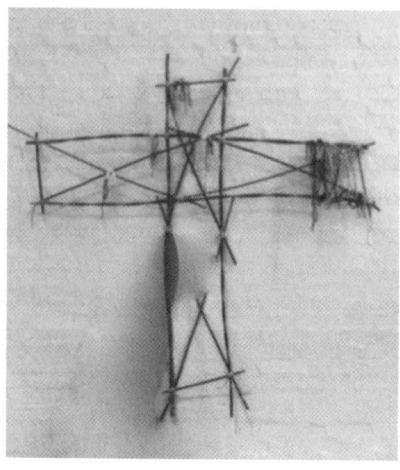

Figure 5: Small willow cross frame used by schoolchildren to help to create the Rag Cross

leftover ribbon, wool from the back of a cupboard. Whatever they brought, it was welcome.

When completed, the school crosses were brought back to the cathedral. There, we assembled them into one giant structure, 16 feet high, hanging at the west end of the cathedral (see Figure 6). It stood tall but familiar, handmade and sacred; its colours layered with meaning. And beside it, we placed these words:

Take these rags,
they are no use to me.
Worn out bits
and rags and stuff.

Ripped and torn
and pulled apart.
Chosen, placed,
and woven in.

Take these rags,
they are no use to me.
Take these rags
and make me beautiful.

Figure 6: The Rag Cross in Sheffield Cathedral

THE PIECES JOIN

Visitors to the cathedral were invited to take a strip of fabric from the rag pile at the base of the cross and tie it on. And they did. Quietly, reverently, people came and added their own thread to the growing body of prayer.

Then, on 22 May, the bombing at the Manchester Arena happened. In the days and weeks that followed, there was a steady stream of people who visited the cathedral. Some came to light candles. Others simply sat in silence. I remember watching people approach the Rag Cross: some visibly grieving; some just still. They sat and stared, picked up a rag and tied it on. No explanation was needed. Something about that cross had become a place to lay down sorrow, to honour pain, to act when there were no words.

I knew enough about trauma to understand, in part, what might be happening. I could see the function the cross was serving: the ritual, the physical act, the invitation to be present in silence, the acknowledgement of the fragmentation and connection. But at that time, I hadn't yet experienced trauma myself. I stood a little outside it, knowing something real was unfolding but not yet knowing it from the inside.

For many victims and survivors of trauma, there is a sense of having been torn apart: physically, emotionally and spiritually. We can long for a type of healing that restores things to how they were, with everything back in its right place, but often our experiences of recovery are more complicated. The metaphors we're offered for healing often fall short. This isn't a jigsaw puzzle in which the pieces will eventually fit neatly back together. It's not about returning to who we were before.

Where we have been torn and ripped, recovery and repair come in different ways. At times, our own threads – our grief, our rage, our silence – are too much to carry alone. The Spirit does not retreat. She stays. Gentle, unflinching and present. Hovering over the rips and tears, over the chaos and silence, where words have run out and strength is thin. She gathers the frayed edges, the torn threads and begins her quiet work of weaving. She stays: gathering what has been torn; reaching for the threads we thought were lost. This is a place where the fragments are gathered in: not fixed or hidden but chosen and held; a space for all that might otherwise be discarded and thrown away.

Recovery, when it comes, often doesn't look like rebuilding. It looks more like joining: a messy, patient, unpredictable joining; a weaving that allows something new to emerge. The pieces don't find a perfect place, but all the pieces are present: the torn threads, the rough edges, the ones that fray and unravel. The movement from ripping to joining is not a straightforward or simple path. It is not about re-forming or patching together what was before, when so much has been lost. Rather, it holds out the hope that joining up the pieces in an altered but recognizable way is possible.

While the path to recovery belongs to the survivor, responsibility for truth and repair belongs with the wider community. The Church bears responsibility for the harm caused and must play its part supporting recovery, standing in solidarity, and working for a safer world and fairer system of justice.

This is the image I see at the heart of the gospel; in Christ, who experienced tearing and breaking, joining and remaking. We speak of a God who stands in solidarity with the oppressed, who binds the wounds of the broken and brings release to those exploited. To speak in this way involves reminding ourselves, over and over again, of where God is and where we as the Church are called to follow, even when the path is painful; even when it asks more from us than we thought we could give.

Bibliography

Abelard, P., 1974, *Ethics: Or 'Know Yourself'*, translated by J. Ramsay, Oxford: Clarendon Press.

Anselm of Canterbury, 1998, *Why God Became Man (Cur Deus Homo)*, translated by J. Hopkins and H. Richardson, London: Penguin Classics (original written c. 1098).

Archbishops' Council, 2000, *Common Worship: Services and Prayers for the Church of England*, London: Church House Publishing.

Archbishops' Council, 2010, *Common Worship: Times and Seasons*, London: Church House Publishing.

Archbishops' Council, 2016, *New Patterns for Worship*, London: Church House Publishing.

Athanasius, 1993, *On the Incarnation*, translated by J. Behr, Crestwood, NY: St Vladimir's Seminary Press (original written c. AD 318–328).

Brown, B., 2013, 'Shame vs. Guilt', *Brené Brown*, 15 January, https://brenebrown.com/articles/2013/01/15/shame-v-guilt (accessed 04.07.2025).

Brown, B., 2021, *Atlas of the Heart*, London: Vermillion.

Campanale, A. (ed.), 2021, 'Mission and Shame', *Anvil: Journal of Theology and Mission*, 37(2), pp. 3–32.

Cherry, S., 2024, *Unforgivable? Exploring the Limits of Forgiveness*, London: SPCK.

Church of England, 2021, *Responding Well to Victims and Survivors of Abuse: Policy and Guidance*, London: House of Bishops, https://www.churchofengland.org/safeguarding/safeguarding-e-manual/responding-well-victims-and-survivors-abuse (accessed 04.07.2025).

Church of England, 2025, 'Redress Scheme', *Church of England*, https://www.churchofengland.org/safeguarding/redress-scheme (accessed 04.07.2025).

Cone, J. H., 2011, *The Cross and the Lynching Tree*, Maryknoll, NY: Orbis Books.

Cross, K., 2020, '"I Have the Power in My Body to Make People Sin": The Trauma of Purity Culture and the Concept of "Body Theodicy"', in K. O'Donnell and K. Cross (eds), *Feminist Trauma Theologies: Body,*

Scripture and Church in Critical Perspective, London: SCM Press, pp. 21–39.

Crown Prosecution Service (CPS), 2023a, 'CPS Annual Report and Accounts, 2022–23', London: Crown Prosecution Service, https://www.cps.gov.uk/publication/cps-annual-report-and-accounts-2022-23 (accessed 30.06.2025).

Crown Prosecution Service (CPS), 2023b, 'Rape Review' dashboard, https://criminal-justice-delivery-data-dashboards.justice.gov.uk/rape-review (accessed 04.09.2025).

Crown Prosecution Service (CPS), 2023c, 'CPS Data Summary Quarter 4, 2022–2023', https://www.cps.gov.uk/publication/cps-data-summary-quarter-4-2022-2023 (accessed 30.06.2025).

DeGruy, J., 2005, *Post Traumatic Slave Syndrome: America's Legacy of Enduring Injury and Healing*, Milwaukie, OR: Uptone Press.

F Word exhibition, June 2022, *The Forgiveness Project*, https://www.theforgivenessproject.com (accessed 04.07.2025).

Gardner, R., 2021, *The Sex Thing: Reimagining Conversations with Young People About Sex*, London: SPCK.

Girard, R., 1977, *Violence and the Sacred*, translated by P. Gregory, Baltimore, MD: Johns Hopkins University Press.

Girard, R., 1986, *The Scapegoat*, translated by Y. Freccero, Baltimore, MD: Johns Hopkins University Press.

Girard, R., 2001, *I See Satan Fall Like Lightning*, New York: Orbis Books.

Herman, J., 2015, *Trauma and Recovery: The Aftermath of Violence – from Domestic Abuse to Political Terror*, reprinted with a new epilogue, New York: Basic Books.

Herman, J. L., 2023, *Truth and Repair: How Trauma Survivors Envision Justice*, New York, NY: Basic Books.

Home Office, 2023, 'Crime Outcomes in England and Wales, 2022 to 2023', *Gov.UK*, London: UK Government, https://www.gov.uk/government/statistics/crime-outcomes-in-england-and-wales-2022-to-2023 (accessed 30.06.2025).

Jamieson, P. D., 2016, *The Face of Forgiveness: A Pastoral Theology of Shame and Redemption*, Downers Grove, IL: IVP Academic.

Janoff-Bulman, R., and Timko, C., 1985, 'Cognitive Biases in Blaming the Victim', *Journal of Experimental Social Psychology*, 21(2), pp. 161–77.

Klein, L. K., 2018, *Pure: Inside the Evangelical Movement that Shamed a Generation of Young Women and How I Broke Free*, New York: Touchstone.

Kolk, B. van der, 2015, *The Body Keeps the Score: Brain, Mind and Body in the Healing of Trauma*, London: Penguin.

Lerner, Melvin J., 1980, *The Belief in a Just World: A Fundamental Delusion – Perspectives in Social Psychology*, New York: Plenum Press.

BIBLIOGRAPHY

Levine, P. A., 1997, *Waking the Tiger: Healing Trauma*, Berkeley, CA: North Atlantic Books.
Lewis, M., 1992, *Shame: The Exposed Self*, New York: Free Press.
McBride, H. L., 2021, *The Wisdom of Your Body: Finding Healing, Wholeness, and Connection through Embodied Living*, Grand Rapids, MI: Brazos Press.
McClintock, K. A., 2011, *Shame-less Lives, Grace-Full Congregations*, Lanham, MD: Rowman & Littlefield.
McNish, J., 2004, *Transforming Shame: A Pastoral Response*, New York: Routledge.
Maté, G., and Maté, D., 2022, *The Myth of Normal: Trauma, Illness, and Healing in a Toxic Culture*, New York: Avery.
Moltmann, J., 1974, *The Crucified God: The Cross of Christ as the Foundation and Criticism of Christian Theology*, London: SCM Press.
Nash, S., 2020, *Shame and the Church: Exploring and Transforming Practice*, London: SCM Press.
Noor, M., and Cantacuzino, M., 2018, *Forgiveness Is Really Strange*, Philadelphia, PA: Singing Dragon.
O'Day, G. R., 2015, 'The Gospel of John', in Leander E. Keck et al. (eds), *Luke, John*, The New Interpreter's Bible Commentary, vol. 8, Nashville, TN: Abingdon Press, pp. 421–742.
Office for National Statistics (ONS), 2023, 'Sexual Offences: Appendix Tables – Year Ending March 2023', *Office for National Statistics*, Newport: ONS, https://www.ons.gov.uk/peoplepopulationandcommunity/crimeandjustice/datasets/sexualoffencesappendixtables (accessed 30.06.2025).
Ogden, P., Minton, K., and Pain, C., 2006, *Trauma and the Body: A Sensorimotor Approach to Psychotherapy*, New York: W. W. Norton & Company.
Origen, 2004, *On First Principles*, translated by G. W. Butterworth, Gloucester, MA: Peter Smith (original early third century).
Partington, M., 2012, *If You Sit Very Still*, London: Jessica Kingsley Publishers.
Partington, M., n.d., 'Stories: Marian Partington', *The Forgiveness Project*, www.theforgivenessproject.com/stories-library/marian-partington (accessed 30.06.2025).
Porges, S. W., and Porges, S., 2023, *Our Polyvagal World: How Safety and Trauma Change Us*, New York: W. W. Norton & Company.
Rambo, S., 2010, *Spirit and Trauma: A Theology of Remaining*, Louisville, KY: Westminster John Knox Press.
Rape Crisis, 'Rape and Sexual Assault Statistics', *Rape Crisis*, https://rapecrisis.org.uk/get-informed/statistics-sexual-violence (accessed 30.06.2025).

Reaves, J. R., Tombs, D., and Figueroa, R. (eds), 2021, *When Did We See You Naked? Jesus as a Victim of Sexual Abuse*, London: SCM Press.

Ross, L., 1977, 'The Intuitive Psychologist and His Shortcomings: Distortions in the Attribution Process', in L. Berkowitz (ed.), *Advances in Experimental Social Psychology*, vol. 10, New York: Academic Press, pp. 173–220.

Rossall, J., 2020, *Forbidden Fruit and Fig Leaves: Reading the Bible with the Shamed*, London: SCM Press.

Schirrmacher, T., 2018, *Culture of Shame/Culture of Guilt: Applying the Word of God in Different Situations*, Eugene, OR: Wipf and Stock.

Tajfel, H., and Turner, J. C., 1979, 'An Integrative Theory of Intergroup Conflict', in W. G. Austin and S. Worchel (eds), *The Social Psychology of Intergroup Relations*, Monterey, CA: Brooks/Cole, pp. 33–47.

Tangney, J. P., and Dearing, R. L., 2003, *Shame and Guilt*, New York: Guildford Press.

Toussaint, L. L., Owen, A. D., and Cheadle, A., 2012, 'Forgive to Live: Forgiveness, Health, and Longevity', *Journal of Behavioural Medicine*, 35(4), pp. 375–86.

Tyndale, W., 2000, *The New Testament*, translated by William Tyndale, facsimile edn (original edn 1530), London: British Library.

Wickham, P., 2023, 'This Is Our God' (song), Fair Trade Services.

You, Y. G., 1997, 'Shame and Guilt Mechanisms in East Asian Culture', *The Journal of Pastoral Care*, 51(1), pp. 57–64.

Further Reading

Church-related abuse

Fife, J., and Gilo (eds), 2019, *Letters to a Broken Church*, London: Ekklesia Publishing.

Graystone, A., 2021, *Bleeding for Jesus: John Smyth and the Cult of the Iwerne Camps*, London: Darton, Longman and Todd.

Harper, R., and Wilson, A., 2019, *To Heal and Not to Hurt: A Fresh Approach to Safeguarding in the Church*, London: Darton, Longman and Todd.

Langberg, D., 2020, *Redeeming Power: Understanding Authority and Abuse in the Church*, Grand Rapids, MI: Brazos Press.

Oakley, L., and Humphreys, J., 2019, *Escaping the Maze of Spiritual Abuse: Creating Healthy Christian Cultures*, London: SPCK.

Stone, S., 2025, *A Heavy Yoke: Theology, Power and Abuse in the Church*, London: SCM Press.

Spiritual practices for survivors

Glasson, B., 2009, *A Spirituality of Survival: Enabling a Response to Trauma and Abuse*, London: A & C Black.

O'Donnell, K., 2024, *Survival: Radical Spiritual Practices for Trauma Survivors*, London: SCM Press.

Trauma theology and the use of biblical texts

Baldwin, J., 2018, *Trauma-Sensitive Theology: Thinking Theologically in the Era of Trauma*, Eugene, OR: Cascade Books.

Boase, E., and Frechette, C. G. (eds), 2016, *Bible through the Lens of Trauma*, Semeia Studies, vol. 86, Atlanta, GA: SBL Press.

Jones, S., 2009, *Trauma and Grace: Theology in a Ruptured World*, Louisville, KY: Westminster John Knox Press.

O'Donnell, K., and Cross, K. (eds), 2020, *Feminist Trauma Theologies: Body, Scripture and Church in Critical Perspective*, London: SCM Press.

Trible, P., 1984, *Texts of Terror: Literary-Feminist Readings of Biblical Narratives*, Philadelphia, PA: Fortress Press.

Violence against women and girls

Bluhm, T., 2021, *Prey Tell: Why We Silence Women Who Tell the Truth and How Everyone Can Speak Up*, Grand Rapids, MI: Brazos Press.

Storkey, E., 2018, *Scars across Humanity: Understanding and Overcoming Violence against Women*, Downers Grove, IL: InterVarsity Press.

Support Organizations

Action on Spiritual Abuse provides support for individuals who have experienced abuse and trauma within faith: www.actionon spiritualabuse.org.uk.

Galop supports LGBTQ+ survivors of abuse: www.galop.org. uk; helpline 0800 999 5428.

Minister and Clergy Sexual Abuse Survivors (MACSAS) supports women and men who have been sexually abused as children or adults by ministers, clergy or others in the Church: www.macsas. org.uk; helpline 0808 801 0340.

Rape Crisis England and Wales offers support and information for women and girls who have experienced sexual violence: www.rapecrisis.org.uk; helpline 0808 500 2222.

Restored is a Christian charity working to raise awareness of domestic abuse, support survivors and equip the Church: www. restored-uk.org.

Safe Spaces offers independent support and advice for anyone who has been abused by someone in the Church of England, Church of Wales or the Catholic Church in England and Wales: www.safespacesenglandandwales.org.uk; helpline 0300 303 1056.

The Survivors Trust is a national umbrella agency for specialist voluntary sector agencies throughout the UK and Ireland. It provides a range of counselling, therapeutic and support services for victims/survivors of rape, sexual violence and sexual abuse: https://thesurvivorstrust.org; helpline 0808 801 0818.

Survivors Voices is a survivor-led organization running peer support groups and survivor gatherings: https://survivorsvoices.org.